Healthy Spirit

First published by Pinion Press 2018
Copyright © 2018 Pinion Press

ISBN
Print: 978-1-925830-37-8
Ebook: 978-1-925830-87-3

Pinion Press has asserted their right under the Copyright, Designs and Patents Act 1988 to be identified as the author of this work. The information in this book is based on the author's experiences and opinions. The publisher specifically disclaims responsibility for any adverse consequences, which may result from use of the information contained herein. Permission to use information has been sought by the author. Any breaches will be rectified in further editions of the book.
All rights reserved. No part of this publication may be reproduced, stored in or introduced into a retrieval system, or transmitted in any form, or by any means (electronic, mechanical, photocopying, recording or otherwise) without the prior written permission of the author. Any person who does any unauthorised act in relation to this publication may be liable to criminal prosecution and civil claims for damages. Enquiries should be made through the publisher.

Cover image: Kev Howlett, Busybird Publishing
Cover design: Busybird Publishing
Layout and typesetting: Nicola Horgan
Editing: Nicola Horgan

Pinion Press
2/118 Para Road
Montmorency, Victoria
Australia 3094
www.busybird.com.au

Pinion Press is an imprint of Busybird Publishing

For every copy of this book sold, $1 will be donated to the Fr Bob Maguire Foundation. To find out about the great work they do, visit: www.fatherbobs.com/

'Man never made any material as resilient as the human spirit.'
— Bernard Williams

Contents

FOREWORD: Light a Candle … *Father Bob*	i
Warrior for the Cause *Jeff 'Joffa' Corfe*	1
Heading in the Rite Direction *Jenny Mitchell*	7
The Soul's Journey of Understanding *Anthony Kilner*	25
How to Love a Lawyer *Arna Delle-Vergini*	49
The Spirit of Yoga *Kylie Hennessy*	65
Beannacht: The Spiritual Care of Irish Blessing *Mary Jo Mc Veigh*	81
The Long Way Home *Eric Hudson*	109
Do What Brings You Joy *Blaise van Hecke*	123
Spirit is as Luminous as Your Awareness *Sally 'Lakshmi Amma' Thurley*	135
Biographies	155

reverend

FOREWORD

Light a Candle for Mercy Against the Darkness of Cruelty

Fr Bob Maguire AM

It is beyond time for us to embrace mercy and kindness if we are to play a part in the development of a gentle, compassionate society.

The Australian culture has had an adulterous affair with money in recent years. There is a growing chasm between the very rich and the very poor. Greed has led to broken homes, street kids, wards of the state, a growing prison population, suicide, and has bankrupted small businesses.

'A fair go' may be as close as many of us gets to mercy. As a national trait it would be a unique spiritual characteristic. Fortunately, there is an Australian spirituality – poverty of spirit – being born. Poverty of spirit means not being attached to worldly goods. Material possessions, popularity, status, learning, health, fitness, physical attractiveness, comfort and security are useful and enjoyable in this life, but they can be abused and become 'gods'.

There is within Australian society a miraculous movement towards reconciliation. Neighbours are encouraged to sort out differences without litigation. Mobile intervention teams are on-call to circumvent the domestic crises. Each of us is called to a spiritual life. Individuals need to learn the skills necessary to discern the spirit at work in daily living. Greed, in one form or another, is the enemy of the spirit. True spirituality includes hospitality towards strangers and, in this fear-ridden society, we all need to be more courageous.

Now, in Australia, there are countless people who are 'just' in the biblical sense, meaning right with God, and who know being good brings its own rewards. It makes life worth living. It gives complete satisfaction. The human heart is made for God, for good, and will not rest until it finds its level.

Each of us needs to review our priorities to ensure that poverty of spirit animates all of us. Spirituality is like a pilgrimage. Religion is like a fortress.

I was moved to design a secular pilgrimage to suit my own neighborhood of Port and South Melbourne. My secular pilgrimage seeks to provide a means by which the area moving and fascinating social landscape might be revealed to all.

The idea is grounded in a reconciliation of the power of pilgrimage, a concept common to large faiths and increasingly finding application in the secular world.

The book *Healthy Spirit* will be a good guide for anyone hitchhiking through the galaxy.

humanitarian

Warrior for the Cause

Jeff 'Joffa' Corfe

Our inner being is guided by our inner spirit. It defines who we are and what we do. I help the homeless because I know firsthand the horrors of being in such a desperate, lonely situation at a young age on the streets of inner city Melbourne. Some people say one person cannot make the world a perfect place, but if more people cared about the plight of others we could make the world a better place. We all have that inner spirit. It just needs nourishing.

People take vitamins to maintain a healthy lifestyle, some will exercise, whilst others eat exceptionally well and/or do both. Keeping the spirit healthy requires daily attention. In my case, I like to help others. Here's one simple way: if you're standing at a supermarket checkout and see a pensioner struggling to pay, offer – with all sincerity – to settle their account.

In the mornings, consider what would be a good thing to do for the day. The nod of the head as we walk past strangers can be uplifting to a person struggling with the negatives of life. A small gesture can be the highlight of that person's day.

Of course, maintaining a healthy spirit is not all about what we can do for others, but watching what kind of things others are doing for the community.

Just recently, the effort in saving eight boys from a flooded cave in the Philippines was food for the spirit. At any Reclink Grand Final, we see great community spirit in helping others connect with each other through sport, which also maintains a healthy lifestyle through friendship and physical activity.

The determination to succeed, to move on and to put bad times behind us, takes time and patience. It's inner spirit that straightens our journey, as well as the understanding that what is now will not be tomorrow.

I am an ambassador for the Epilepsy Foundation because I have a daughter with epilepsy. I have so much appreciation for these people because they keep moving forward, refusing to let this horrible illness shape their lives. They have that spirit to focus on what lies ahead, and that spirit is contagious. Watching anyone do good for their fellow citizen inspires the inner spirit.

Let me explain: some days are good, some are not.

You know on the not-so-good days you're doing okay if you can still put yourself ahead of your own feelings for the sake of others. This is a wonderful gift that arises from a healthy spirit, to be touched by the sadness of others, and acknowledge their hardships with empathy and compassion. To walk in another person's shoes to get a better perspective grows a healthy inner spirit. It is a cliché but true: treat others how you would like to be treated. Sacrifice your mood or thoughts for the betterment of others. Have purpose, strength and courage – what wonderful ingredients in times of adversity! Listen to yourself. Question yourself by seeking your inner spirit, and being at peace with yourself and others.

Be a warrior for the cause.

celebrant

Heading in the Rite Direction

Jenny Mitchell

About fifteen years ago my grandfather, Tom, shared some wisdom with me just before I moved away from home to take up my first real job.

'Jenny, you need to be like Sister Maria,' he said.

I was twenty-two and so naturally I thought, *Holy fuck! He wants me to be a nun?*

Fortunately, he went on to explain that he was referring to Julie Andrews' irrepressible and spunky character in *The Sound of Music*. Tom wanted me to channel her and her self-assured refrain *I have confidence in … me!* as I went off to my new adventure.

Smart guy, is Tom.

Ironically, two years later, I became a civil marriage celebrant and often found myself mistaken for a priest.

As a celebrant (though definitely not a priestly one), I've reflected on the role that ceremonies and rituals play in contemporary Australians' lives. A familiar view is that non-religious Australians do not 'do' ceremonies, except for weddings and funerals – and even then we only tolerate them until we can get to the eating and drinking part.

Another perspective is that we might consider popular holidays like Christmas – with all its trimmings – to be 'ritualistic' even if we are not religious: think decorated Christmas trees, gift-giving, Christmas stockings, and the endless yuletide reruns of *Love Actually*.

These sorts of ceremonies and rituals are generally accepted because they are connected to the institutions that our society respects: marriage, death and public holidays!

Traditional ceremonies – such as weddings and funerals – continue to be commonplace, however, civil celebrants – rather than religious ministers – increasingly conduct them.

Baby-naming ceremonies (a sort of secular version of a christening) have been growing in popularity, although they still tend to be eclipsed by extravagant first birthday parties.

And have you noticed how graduation ceremonies have ballooned in recent years? Once they were a staple for universities and occasionally Year 12 but, nowadays, young parents find themselves attending Grade 6 graduations, Prep graduations, and even kinder or pre-school graduations.

It seems to me that modern Australians appreciate the role of ceremony and ritual perhaps more than they realise.

A place for ceremony and ritual in contemporary, secular Australia

Can there be something entirely modern, socially acceptable, decidedly normal – or even *cool* – about ceremonies and ritual in the lives of all Australians?

You may already find you have ceremony and ritual in your everyday life, even if you are non-religious. After all, these activities are ubiquitous – so much so that we barely recognise them as rituals.

Do any of these rituals sound familiar?

- Singing 'Happy Birthday', blowing out the candles, and cutting the cake
- Showering mothers-to-be with nursery gifts and pamper packs, and playing games to guess the baby's gender
- Having a barbecue on Australia Day
- Buying a 'democracy sausage' at the local primary school on Election Day
- Family and friends making speeches at an 18th or 21st birthday
- That older friend who sends a Christmas letter every year, detailing the activities and exploits of themselves and their family over the past twelve months
- Laying down of time capsules at schools

- The whole gamut of rituals and traditions at Christmas and Easter time, regardless of religion

Have you been to any of these ceremonies?

- Sporting clubs' prize and trophy nights
- The opening and closing Olympic ceremonies
- A renewal of marriage vows
- Membership ceremonies at clubs, or the swearing in of office-bearers
- Sod-turning ceremonies for the construction of a new community building
- Adoption ceremonies
- 'Christening' or naming of boats or ships
- Citizenship ceremonies for new Australians
- ANZAC Day and Remembrance Day services.

More familiar rites of passage fit in here too: weddings, funerals, anniversaries, graduations and baby-naming ceremonies.

There are other rituals too, which once seemed new and strange but have become commonplace – like the Welcome to Country often included at the beginning of presentations, speeches and conferences.

Ceremonies and rituals give us common meaning as a community and as a broader society. They help us to celebrate milestones, pause and reflect on accomplishments, and, together, set aspirations for the future.

What are 'ceremonies' and 'rituals'?

The terms themselves can mean different things to different people, and can conjure up anything from a traditional church wedding to one of those faux-pagan rites that moody teenagers like to dabble in after a short internet search. At their heart, however, ceremonies and rituals often have a lot in common, despite the differences in the societies and communities that perform them.

They are, for example, often combined with an occasion of some sort. They express certain sentiments or commitments, or convey a rite of passage. There must undoubtedly be some meaning to them, at least as far as the group involved is concerned.

And they are *usually* undertaken by a group of people, or by an individual in the presence of a group – a group connected in some way, be it family, friends, or members of an association of some kind.

There are frequently procedures or observances involved and are often inclusive of something symbolic: a gesture, representation, costume or other visual cue.

Some ceremonies and rituals are solemn, some joyous and fun, and others reflective or nostalgic. Some might even just be an awkward political stunt, but those have their place too.

What do ceremonies and rituals do for us?

There are many ways ceremonies and rituals can make us spiritually richer.

Pausing to reflect, and to celebrate

Ceremonies and rituals provide perfect opportunities to reflect and to celebrate milestones and achievements. As any management consultant will tell you, taking the time to celebrate successes is critical for good morale and a shared sense of purpose.

Celebratory ceremonies and rituals are easy to bring to mind. From the big ones like weddings, birthdays, and baby-gender reveals, to the lesser rituals of your first solo drive after getting your licence or celebratory drinks for that promotion at work.

A guy I knew at university had a celebratory ritual of shaving off his beard at the end of an exam period. I assume the ritual invoked a sense of freedom for him or perhaps the beard just symbolised a 'hairy' time for him!

A sense of belonging through connection to family, community and place
There is also no doubt that a sense of belonging and connection can nurture one's spirit. Rituals in families abound: where, what and how dinner is served; morning routines; holiday activities; how birthdays and other occasions are observed; and the ritual of visiting extended family. All of these serve to connect us to the people in our 'tribe'. Formal ceremonies can go beyond family, connecting us to a network of people sharing the same community, beliefs, or place.

The sand ceremony – popular at weddings – is symbolic of individuals mixing together to form something new. The idea is that the granules of different sands, once poured into the same vessel, can't ever be separated again, much like a family that's been bonded together in marriage.

Aspirations and wishes for a wonderful future
Ceremonies and rituals can be a chance to pronounce aspirations for the future – from bestowing wishes on a baby, to exchanging vows in a marriage renewal ceremony, to making commitments to uphold certain behaviours and ethics upon being sworn into office.

As any goal-setter will attest, making your commitments known to others makes you profoundly more likely to achieve them.

I know a bride and groom who truly made the ritual of exchanging wedding rings their own. The groom was a tradie and not one for wearing jewellery.

The bride therefore instead presented him with the mountain bike he'd always wanted, complete with the following vow: 'With this bike, I thee wed. It is a strong bike ready for any adventure, sunshine or rain. It demonstrates the infinite energy, passion and fun that will fill our married lives.' They are just about to celebrate their tenth wedding anniversary and will renew their vows in front of family and friends.

Leaving a legacy
Sometimes, a person or a generation may feel it's important that they are a leaving a legacy. Examples of this are when a person endows an institution like a school or university, or when a tree is planted in memoriam or for some other symbolic purpose.

A popular inclusion in wedding ceremonies nowadays is a short ritual whereby the bride and groom lay down a bottle of wine and love letters to each other in a small wooden box, which they nail shut during the ceremony. The idea is that they will open it on a significant anniversary or other milestone (perhaps even with their future children).

Certainly, feeling that you are making a contribution to, or will be remembered by, another set of newcomers – be they descendants, members of your community, or even your future self – can be good for your existential soul.

Rites of passage
Why are so many of us excited by all the details of a celebrity or royal wedding (apart from wanting to see what Posh Spice is wearing)? Is it the feeling that they are just the same as us when they perform common rituals?

Perhaps it's that there's something nice about seeing them break down the walls of duty and formality to reveal what they really are – a couple in love. It is something we can relate to, a familiar rite of passage. So too is graduation, or the birth of a baby. Rites of passage are often milestones common to the human experience, worthy of commemoration and celebration in the name of a healthy spirit.

A friend of mine and her siblings were all subjected to their parents' ritual of unexpectedly turning up for dinner when they first moved out of home. The parents claimed it was a test to see if they could manage impromptu entertaining, complete with food and a clean house. In their family, that was a sign of adulthood. The kids all hated it at the time, but now they love recounting their experiences with much laughter. Each of them has vowed to do the same thing to their own children.

Where to from here?

Would it seem awkward to have everyone stop talking, laughing, eating and drinking at a birthday party and 'have a ceremony'? Would your friends think you wildly indulgent (or suspect marital troubles) if you decided to renew your vows?

Can participating in such ceremonies and rituals benefit our spiritual life and nurture a healthy spirit? Undoubtedly so. How do you feel after you've been to a wedding? How do you feel at a birthday party? How do you feel at a graduation? Joyful? Proud? Like you belong?

I'm not advocating a change in the way we do things, the way we go about our celebrations or our time spent with loved ones, but to be mindful and present so that when we do engage in ceremony and ritual, we recognise and acknowledge the spiritual nurturing in which we're indulging.

Health experts will tell you to eat mindfully so you experience all the sensations of your food. Likewise, mental health experts will tell you to practise gratefulness – taking the time to identify and acknowledge all that there is to feel thankful for in the here and now. Similarly, the next time you sing 'Happy Birthday', look around at who is present and see how they are feeling.

Take stock of the fact that you are collectively participating in that moment and consider what you are gaining – positive rites of passage, celebrating and reflecting on achievement, a sense of belonging, shared aspirations for the future, and the joy of spending time with loved ones.

Who knows? You may want to make those experiences richer – plan for them, decide on just the right words to make them even more special, discuss with others the meaning they have for you, and maybe, just maybe, even consider having that baby-naming ceremony or renewing your vows. So my challenge to you if you want to use ceremony and ritual to fuel a healthy spirit:

- Be mindful
- Acknowledge meaning
- Make a memory.

Here's an idea
Australians love a house renovation. We're mad for watching home makeover shows, buying property we can't afford, flipping something outrageously seventies into something definitively now (dressed up in K-mart home couture, of course). Arguably, it's all in search of the Australian Dream: the *forever home*.

So how about if you or someone close to you actually finds, builds, remodels, extends, and finally finishes their forever home, you celebrate that huge achievement with a ceremony?

Bring family and friends together. Choose someone to officiate. Think about what you want to say: maybe you could reflect upon, applaud, express gratitude for, and acknowledge the stress and sacrifice that has gone into the huge project. Talk about what the house actually *means* to you, and to your family. What does it represent? What do you dream your future looks like in your new home?

Have a think about some symbolism: perhaps your celebrant could perform a 'home blessing'? Maybe you'd like to plant a tree to grow as your house matures? You could bury a time capsule in the backyard. How would such a ceremony feel for you?

I'm willing to bet (not the house of course, but a small amount) that everyone in attendance would feel at least a little spiritually nurtured.

And a final thought
My son, Kit, recently had his first birthday. On the advice of his big sister, three-year-old Ginger, we had an animal-themed party and invited our family and a few friends. There was a big dinosaur cake, balloons, party games, and lots of food.

There was also something else. We explained to Ginger that we were going to hold a 'wish ceremony' and, just like the fairies did for Princess Aurora in *Sleeping Beauty*, everyone was going to bring wishes for baby Kit. When our guests arrived, we asked everyone to write a wish for Kit on a special card and drop it in a little box. Guests could write their name on the wish, or leave it anonymous.

My husband and I had also spent some time thinking about some words we wanted to share with our loved ones and some elements of a naming ceremony we wanted to incorporate as part of the celebration. The ceremony itself took only about ten minutes, but it was a little more than making a speech, and we then had the beautiful cards as keepsakes to treasure for Kit.

It went something like this:

> Kit's dad: 'First off I just wanted to welcome everyone and thank you all for coming today to celebrate Kit's first birthday. Jen and I thought it was a great opportunity to have a little bit of a wish ceremony for Kit, and so thank you all for writing your wishes for Kit on the cards. We'll get to those in a moment.
>
> 'We wanted to say a little bit about Kit's name and why we chose it. Jen was a huge fan of *The Phantom* as a child (she inherited this from her mum). "Kit Walker" is the name used by the Phantom when he is travelling incognito. I loved watching the TV series *Knight Rider* with my dad when I was growing up. But we didn't think we could call him "Hasselhoff"!

'Kit's middle name is Aleksander, using the Polish spelling with a K and an S, rather than an X. He is given this name from his great-great-grandfather on Jen's side. We understand that Aleksander was an amazing man and dad.

'Of course, we're not the first parents to want to call our son Kit. There are a few famous Kits out there. Fans of *Game of Thrones* will be familiar with the actor Kit Harrington, who plays Jon Snow. Others may remember Kit Cloudkicker – a cartoon character from the nineties early morning cartoon series, *Tailspin*. And, of course, there was Kit Marlowe – the famous playwright and contemporary of Shakespeare. It was Marlowe who wrote, "There is no sin but ignorance."

'Kit also shares his birthday with others, including the Russian actor Yul Brenner, Italian fashion designer Giorgio Armani, and, our favourite of all, former Australian Prime Minister Gough Whitlam. Incredibly, Kit's sister Ginger was born on the day Whitlam died, so we can only assume there is a spiritual connection between our kids and old Gough.

'Now, it's on to what we wish for him. His mum and I would like to wish him a life full of happiness, laughter and pleasant surprises. Jen will read out what you have all wished for Kit.'

I proceeded to read out everyone's cards – about thirty of them. Everyone had a good laugh, with the occasional 'awww'. The cards included everything from wishing Kit 'pancakes every morning' (his nine-year-old cousin) to wishing that anyone who meets him will think, *Wow what a boy!* (his ninety-five-year-old great-grandfather).

Yep, that would be Tom. Smart guy.

psychic medium

The Soul's Journey of Understanding

Anthony Kilner

> 'Everyone has a spirit that can be refined, a body that can be trained in some manner, a suitable path to follow. You are here to realise your inner divinity and manifest your innate enlightenment.'
>
> – Morihei Ueshiba

As a Psychic Medium, my world offers amazing insights into being an energy source in a physical body having a human experience – or to put it another way, our human body being the vessel for our energy, our soul, and our spirit.

But what exactly is our spirit? Over the years I have come across a lot of confusion as to the difference between a soul, the spirit body or higher self, and the spirit.

The soul, spirit and spirit body are different things. Understanding the differences can be confusing, although the concept is simple, and sometimes discussion on these topics is more complicated than it needs to be. My thoughts transcend religious beliefs and are more aligned to creating the perfect union of mind, body and spirit within each of us, with the ultimate aim of being or becoming an enlightened being.

This is a spiritual journey for us in our physical body – a journey of understanding, garnering knowledge in this life, and in the multiple lives we lead, or will lead, or are living concurrently.

It's the soul's journey to understand the darkness that shrouds our physical lives that affects our soul. To have a healthy spirit, a healthy soul, we need to understand the darkness that feeds us.

> 'One does not become enlightened by imagining figures of light, but by making the darkness conscious.'
>
> – Carl Jung

Light Exists in Darkness

What is the darkness? The darkness is war, the killing of humans and animals, plants and our planet in general. It's hard to understand why a conscious, enlightened being would even go there.

But we do.

This planet is here for the benefit of everyone who has lessons to learn about darkness. Once these lessons are understood, we will move on to an enlightened Plane of Existence in furtherance of our own soul's journey.

In esoteric terms, a Plane of Existence refers to a level or state of consciousness that can be reached with the mind rather than the physical body. We live on the Earth Plane in a physically conscious state of mind with a relatively low vibrational energy field. The Astral Realm is a Plane of Higher Consciousness that requires a higher vibration of our spirit body to reach. We achieve this higher vibration in sleep state when our spirit body leaves the physical body and journeys to the various Astral Realms. These Astral Realms can also be reached through meditation.

Leaving this Earth Plane behind allows every living thing on this planet to evolve in its own time, and to make its own choices for good or bad.

However, living on a planet that is being destroyed by so called self-righteous people (often under the banner of religious dogma) is abhorrent. Governments feel they have the right to control our populations by force and/or mind control. There are many examples of this, such as the annexation of Tibet by China, and what's happening in many states of Africa with the sheer number of displaced people escaping corrupt governments and warmongers. One country fights to control another with the subsequent wars, rape, famine, torture and death that come with subjugating people.

Look at some of the leaders of today: Donald Trump, Vladimir Putin, Xi Jinping and Kim Jong-un, as well as oil barons, war lords and chieftains who are so engaged in trying to look after themselves and their growing country's greed, that they cause hardship for others. How many wars are fought in the so-called name of freedom that have destroyed the souls and spirits of the living, and the dead?

Even here, in Australia, politicians and other greedy people are more interested in lining their own pockets than genuinely helping those in need. How can the greedy freely give themselves a pay rise and perks when so many people live below the poverty line?

Add religion and fundamentalism into the mix. How much soul-destroying work has been done in the name of God over the last 2000-odd years and the eons before that? An evil pall of energy hangs over the world, shrouding thousands of souls. Think of the Crusades, the war between the north and the south of the Americas and the conquering of indigenous peoples in many countries.

So can this planet change – I mean *really* change? Part of me says no, because it's a planet based on FEAR. From our days of *kill-or-be-killed*, we have lived in fear. We are ANIMALS that have a conscious thought program that has allowed us to create a society around materialism and the ability to *'smite the weak – to dominate as all animal species do!'* Part of me says NO because we still have nations at war. Nothing has really changed on this planet during its history of so-called, conscious thinking HUMANITY.

FEAR is what the media are trained in. It sells. FEAR is what drives us to take up arms and barricade ourselves in our homes. FEAR is what creates bullies and dictators. FEAR is what allows governments to rule populations.

FEAR is what we are taught to believe from birth and that if we kill or destroy the ones we FEAR we are somehow better, or stronger, which allows us to instil FEAR into others to keep us at the top of the food chain.

FEAR of death is another form of darkness that needs to be overcome to reach enlightenment. In many communities, death is not always addressed with respect and understanding. Because many religious beliefs instill fear of going to hell or purgatory (both referred to as Planes of Existence in religious terms), or coming back as a bug as in Buddhism, people often fear what happens when we die.

In my world, this planet we live on is HELL and there's nothing underneath the Earth that we go to when we die if we have been bad. A place where our soul is tortured to the very end of days – I mean, really! How FEAR-driven is that religious dogma?

Because of conditioning by family and friends, sceptics, or people who simply don't believe in anything, are scared of dying. Others might be frightened of what might happen to them, their families, their loved ones and their pets once they go.

In many ways the human condition is to love and protect. In understanding that, can we do this journey without judgement and fear? It could be a foreign concept for many, especially for the martyrs out there.

Simply put, FEAR destroys souls and conquers people's spirits. FEAR does not liberate anyone on this planet. By understanding the truth of what fear is, our souls can be set free.

> 'A mind unruffled by the vagaries of fortune, from sorrow freed, from defilements cleansed, from fear liberated — this is the greatest blessing.'
>
> – The Buddha, (Mangala Sutta).

Inspiration Brings Love

On the other side of the FEAR coin, there are some truly inspirational people who have helped this planet survive as long as it has. These people – through compassion, technology, wealth, and even religion – all offer some light at the end of the FEAR tunnel.

Overcoming their own FEAR has offered a path forward for thousands of people over many generations. Finding a way through FEAR is the best way to create a healthy spirit and therefore a healthy soul.

These people, all now in the spirit world, are too numerous to mention. Some include Ghandi, the Dalai Lama, the Pope (as an office rather than a man), Fred Hollows AC, and Buddha.

Then there are amazing musicians in modern times such as Prince, John Denver, Jim Morrison, as well as actors and comedians such as Robin Williams and Graham Kennedy. They have all helped raise the spirits of many people living in adversity and fear.

These people changed other people's lives and many fought hard against such spirit-destroying things like governments, drugs, alcohol, mental health conditions and the conditioning of others.

Of course, many people are standing up in our lifetime – people such as Russell Brand, Olivia Newton-John, Kylie Minogue, Delta Goodrem and Deepak Chopra. They are spreading their own words of awakening and support for people with mental and physical issues, and they are helping people fight FEAR by empowering their spirit and their soul.

But it's the everyday families that have struggled with illness, adversity, death and horror, that are our biggest teachers for creating a positive, healthy spirit.

There are many people like Rosemary (Rosie) Batty – Rosie has devoted years of her life to this task and has potentially saved thousands from domestic abuse.

Daniel Morcombe's parents, Bruce and Denise, have been through such anguish and adversity, yet if they have inspired and raised awareness in the populace so that one person can be saved from abduction and murder, they will be grateful. They have a spirit that wants to live on, a beautiful soul that wants to help humanity.

Whether it's religion as we know it, spiritualism (as I believe in it, as a philosophy aligning with Buddhism), scepticism, or simply a zest for life, it doesn't matter what you believe in, you can find a path through the darkness.

As long as you don't tell others what to believe or, create FEAR as a basis for life, then there is always hope for people's spirit to live on and be healthy. This, in turn, helps create a healthy body for their soul to reside in.

The more we bring joy and love into the world, the more chance it has of shifting a FEAR-based planet to a LOVE-based planet.

Let's explore the differences between our soul and our spirit amongst many other questions with the intent that there is a way to create a *Healthy Spirit!*

> 'The path to pain free enlightenment starts by walking inside the body, through the heart and into the soul. Stepping through the fear and conditioning since birth that surrounds the soul. This act relives and relieves the pain of life's journey through passive understanding.'
>
> – Anthony Kilner 2018.

Soul Understanding

What is the difference between a Soul and a Spirit and a Spirit Body?

The soul is the life force that infuses our body. It also connects us to our soul collective. It's easy to refer to the soul as the spirit of a person, but I believe the spirit of the person is based around the mind, while the soul is based on the energy within, hence the trinity – mind, body, spirit.

There is also the spirit body – often referred to as our etheric body. This is our energetic body, which mirrors our physical body and travels to and through the various Astral Realms or Planes of Existence.

In our dream state our spirit body can travel around the globe and it can gather information to help us move through life. This body offers us mere humans a way to connect to all things on this world and on others.

Some people refer to the spirit body as the Higher Self, but in my way of thinking the Higher

Self is our soul which is connected to our Soul Collective.

The Soul Collective is where the souls of all our lives lived or will live, congregate, gather, and merge.

In essence, we have a physical body powered by an energy system that houses our soul. We also have a spiritual body, which is a part of the energetic system that is also connected to our soul and the physical body.

Then we have spirit, which is of the mind and comes from the brain. This affects our energy levels and therefore affects our ability to live healthily in both the physical and spiritual sense.

This insightful book is titled *Healthy Spirit*. However, on this spiritual level it could have been called *Healthy Soul* quite easily.

Soul Principles
Our physical body is a bunch of cells, organs, bones, fluids and the like, and requires energy to power it.

Much like a car, power is needed to get the motor going – the battery and ECU – and our electrical systems manage this process.

This is handled via our chakra system, which generates our auric field and our subtle bodies.

These diagrams show the seven major chakras and the related subtle bodies and the related Planes of Existence.

The Soul's Journey of Understanding

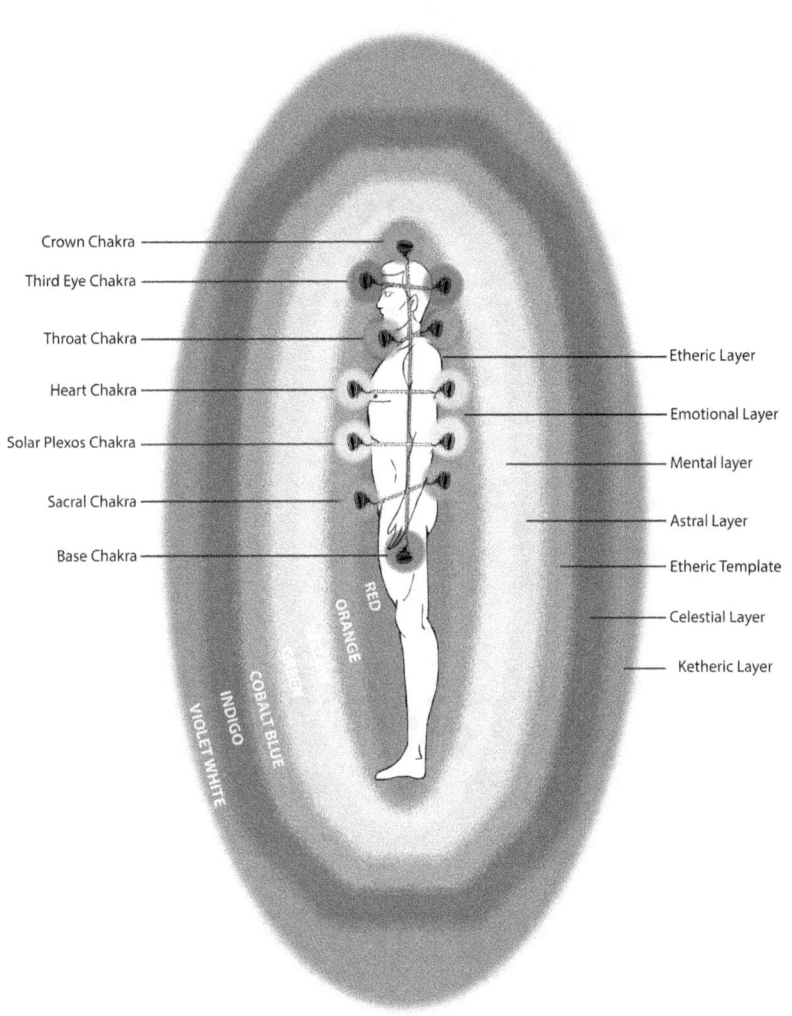

Healthy Spirit

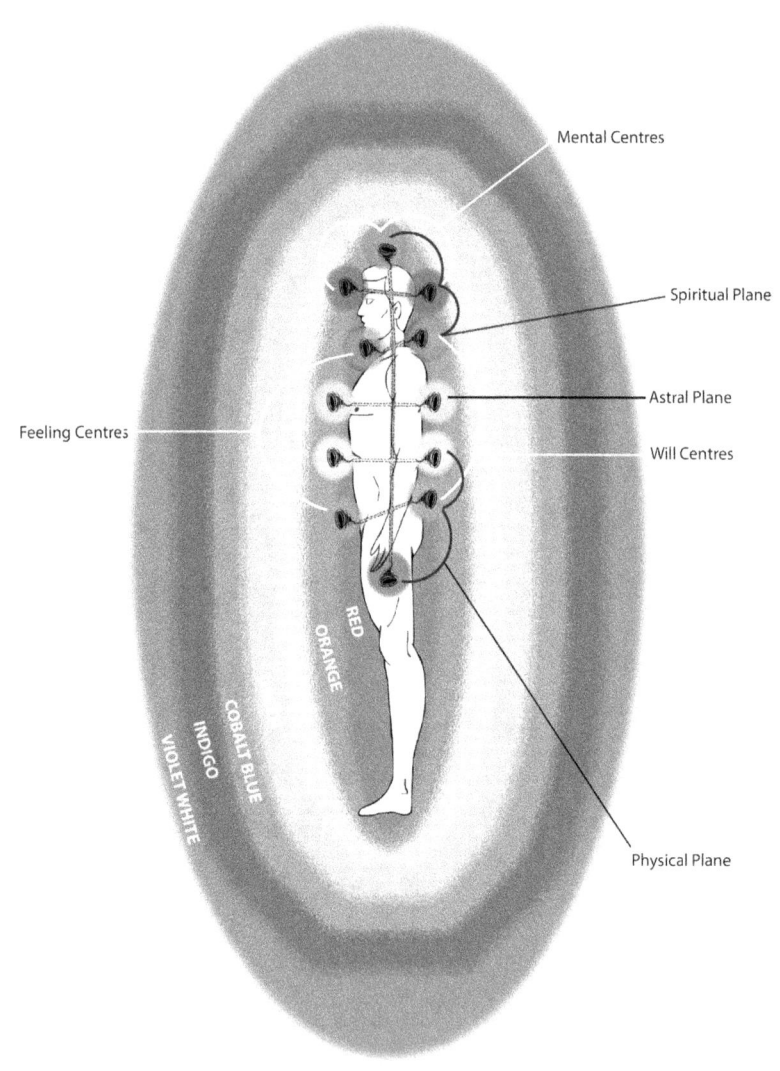

Energy travels through the physical body via energy lines, referred to as *nadis* and *meridians*. This energy movement keeps us alive.

Like any vehicle, it won't run properly if there is no fuel or the fuel is bad. If we put crap into our body then it will break down eventually. If something mechanical breaks, the car stops. If we break bones, have hereditary disease and so on, then the body stops also.

If we don't look after our body then it dies.

The soul is the driver of this vehicle. The soul relies on the engine to run smoothly, which means it relies on the vehicle's electricals – the brain – to get from A to B. The cooling system is our emotions, while the power and torque of the engine provides the brawn – our physical muscle.

But where does the soul reside in all this? The expression 'the eyes are the window to the soul' is apt as we can look into another's soul through each other's eyes and we can use a mirror to see our soul through our own eyes, although I believe the soul resides in the heart space – the centre of our chest. From there, it infuses our whole body. It's the energy source for everything our human body needs to survive.

In the soul's journey we rely on others to help keep the vehicle moving safely and reliably. Sometimes, though, we can get lost or damaged by others, therefore changing our intended journey. That's when the challenges start. This is where our spirit's will to live kicks in and that's a product of the mind affecting the soul.

Some years ago I read an interesting reflection on war and death that reported how some people died from minor wounds while others survived the most horrific of wounds. Why? The writer thought that some people's spirit drove the will to live and, because the soul had not yet completed its journey, they were not yet ready to die. Our fighting spirit wants to live, our soul wants to complete its journey, yet without that good fight, we die.

The interesting thing is that our soul's journey is known to the soul and everything that happens to us in life happens for a reason. By accepting that and trusting that a higher purpose is involved, we start our amazing path to enlightenment.

This path alone is scary because it means living in the moment and trying not to react to our humanness. It means letting go of ego, attachment, and fear, and accepting that if we follow our truth then the path will unfold before us – like I said, it's a scary path to walk!

The Spirit Body
Our spirit body is connected to our physical body and the earth via an energy-based silver cord. When we die, that cord is severed, which releases our soul to return to the soul collective.

Our spirit body has the ability to travel through time and space, inter-dimensionally and across the various Planes of Existence. There is not one Plane of Existence: it's planes within planes – a Multiverse is a better word to describe it.

There are many reasons for this sort of astral travel: to learn, to play, to teach and to share experiences with all manner of beings from other times and places.

This is another way that we can learn from others while our physical body sleeps. There are plenty of people out there who have mastered the art of astral travelling while awake too – via a deep meditative state. This takes time and discipline, yet it's very achievable even if many think it impossible.

The more we open our minds to our soul and to our spirit, the more we realise that everything without is within, the sooner we'll realise there's a way forward to create a healthy spirit. If we consider this statement, the diagrams make even more sense because each chakra is related to a different subtle body, which in fact is a Plane of Existence. Everything we need to heal, to be happy and to have a healthy spirit, is within us.

The Soul Collective
One train of thought suggests we live a linear life. We start life in one year and die X amount of years later. We then go to some place, a place in

the Astral Realm, where our lives are collated and understood by our soul and our Soul Collective. We are then reborn later in that linear time frame.

I understand our lives are based on a Quantum Consciousness theory – we are living a range of lives in different time periods all at the same time. Our Soul Collective is where we can share our collective experiences from each life, and share information from different lives to help us grow and learn on a soul level.

How many times have inventors, writers, doctors and other people been experiencing a problem and then the light bulb lights up? Where did that information come from? God, guides, the universe or some higher energy, or was it a message from the Soul Collective because it was time that a solution needed to be revealed for that problem?

Imagine a person's soul is experiencing a life in another time period where a problem had been solved. Imagine that the soul from that period, now connected through the Soul Collective, shared the solution to that problem, hence the light bulb moment.

Messages from the Soul Collective can and do come through like that, as well as in our dreams. Messages from the Soul Collective travel via our Super Consciousness to our Subconscious where we then start processing it in our Conscious State. Most people understand the Conscious State as the state of being awake and functioning.

Our Subconscious is the filing system of the mind that holds all our memories, bringing them up when we need them and even sometimes when we don't want them. The Super Consciousness is like a telecommunications link to our Soul Collective which transmits messages from our past and future lives.

Dreams and messages require interpretation to understand. Carl Jung talks about an Unconscious Consciousness, whereby we are all connected via some universal connectedness that allows us to understand symbology in pictures as a shared language rather than words.

Hieroglyphs are one ancient example of this, while male and female signs, toilet signs, stop signs are other fairly universal symbols out there. I think Jung was on to something because we all understand pictures from around the world where we certainly don't understand all the world's languages.

Take this a step further and reflect on the Soul Collective and how many concurrent lives are running in multiple languages in a variety of time periods, countries, Planes of Existence and other worlds where the universal leveller is communication by pictures. This is also why the information shared this way usually needs interpretation.

Creating A Healthy Soul, A Healthy Spirit, A Healthy Body

> 'Your spiritual journey starts with a 180 degree turn backwards. This way you can see how far your journey has been. It also provides a measure for the next step forward into your truth!'
>
> – Anthony Kilner 2012.

Knowledge, time, love and a sacred space are the four ingredients necessary to create a healthy spirit. Healthy Spirit is, not coincidentally, the third in the Health Conscious Series: Mind, Body and Spirit.

In *Healthy Mind* the chapters all offer help to get the mind going in the right direction. My chapter covered meditation techniques and vibrational energy work with a spiritual bent, getting the mind in the right space.

Meditation is not as hard as many people think. Set aside some time every day to listen to some peaceful music and allow your mind to go blank, or concentrate on one topic to the exclusion of all others to find a solution to a problem.

With patience, time and practice, this skill will allow the practitioner to start soaring through the skies, Planes of Existence and open their awareness to another world through a soul connection.

In *Healthy Body*, the authors offered various techniques and ways to get the body into shape. My chapter dealt with the metaphysics of the body that require interpretation to understand that the body never lies – body pain or a condition leads us to a subjective understanding of a way to fix the body or understand a way forward in life. This can also help people understand the way the body and the mind are linked with the soul and the Soul Collective.

The next step is to create a sacred space. This special space is where a person can feel safe and be at peace every time they go there. This space may include room for sharing the experience with a loved one, alive or in spirit world, as this journey can and will be an emotional one.

In this sacred space – and with love being your main thought – allow your mind to drift back to each event in your life that you still harbour anger or resentment for, and examine this event objectively. One way to do this is to write each experience down in a book. Record all the emotions around the event with as much detail as you can manage. Then start the meditation on one page/event at a time.

Look at each event from all sides – from a young person's point of view, from an old person's point of view, and from your own point of view. See yourself as the perpetrator as well as the victim. This technique will allow you to understand the event with clarity and also understand how that one event shaped your journey in regard to other events.

This is going to be hard and empowering. There could be tears, frustration, anger, fear, but above all, there needs to be self-understanding and LOVE in the process. *TIME = LOVE!* Give yourself time and love to make this journey special.

By going through this process one event at a time – and with total objectivity – your path will become clearer. These events will then become road signs in your life's direction. Only then can true empathy reflect who you are – a person who comes from the heart without fear or judgement.

> 'We are all on our path – no further ahead nor behind others. And who can honestly say they are further ahead or behind others without judging?'
>
> - Anthony Kilner, 2017.

Creating a healthy spirit – a healthy soul – will challenge even the best of us. In many cases, life gets too hard, it gets too busy and it gets scary to move forward with any clarity and often the question is asked, *Why am I here?*

It's at this point that a doorway will appear and also the rabbit hole. Falling down the rabbit hole tends to be the long way around to finding oneself, while it's often harder to open and step through the doorway. Yet opening the door is a more controlled way to proceed forward and expand the mind, body and soul.

Either way you decide to go, there is always a soloution and a way forward for brave and fearless souls to journey.

lawyer

How to Love a Lawyer
(even when you are one)

Arna Delle-Vergini

It's hard to love yourself at the best of times. When you're a lawyer, it's doubly hard. There are a myriad of reasons why it is hard to love yourself when you are a lawyer and it is impossible, of course, to capture them all here, but let's start with a few obvious ones.

Firstly, a lot of people don't like you and some don't feel obligated to hide it either. Ever wondered who makes up all those really bad lawyer jokes? The answer is 'people'.

People make up those really bad lawyers jokes, such as this gem …

> Q: *What do you call fifty lawyers lying at the bottom of the ocean?*
> A: *A good start.*

Excuse me a moment while I laugh uproariously. I've only heard this about a thousand times.

People don't just make up bad lawyer jokes, they relish telling them and the reason why they relish telling them is because, for the most part, *they don't much like lawyers!*

Secondly, you argue for a living. Every. Single. Day. Want to live in a constant state of hyperarousal in an environment where you are despised, feared, bullied, and sometimes revered all at the same time?

Well, the courtroom is the work environment for you.

If you are particularly attached to constant inescapable and brutal conflict, then I recommend the courtrooms customarily hearing criminal, family, children, or family violence matters. Why not ramp it up and practise in all of the above areas? You know, for added effect. There is nothing that quite says, 'I am a good person. I am worthy. I am loved and I am appreciated', more than a job where you engage in bitter and protracted arguments for a living.

Like holidays or even short breaks? Please don't become a lawyer. The lawyer who lives a leisurely, restful and balanced life is either retired or in the latter stages of recovering from a complete breakdown.

That's not to say lawyers don't strive for work/life balance. Work/life balance is the mantra of the last *at least* eight or so years. Pity no one can really explain what it means, let alone hope to show us how to live by its precepts.

In the meantime, while greater minds are trying to figure it all out, the rest of us keep toiling, day-to-day at the interminable grindstone of Law and Justice.

Hanging out with a tense, uptight and overworked lawyer is unlikely to be high on most people's list of having 'a good time'. It certainly isn't high on our own lists of how to have a good time so I sympathise completely.

Last but not least, when you practise Law you come across all that is broken in this world. Just walk into any courtroom on any day and you will see broken people. You will see suffering, cruelty, abuse of power, discrimination, negligence and fraud.

You will see the very worst of people and at some point you will start to see the potential for the very worst *in everyone you meet* – whether they are associated with court or not – for the simple reason that they are, well, people and if they are people then they are capable of the very worst of human behaviour.

This is when it gets horrifying. Eventually you come to another realisation: *you* are also a person and thus, *even you* are capable of the very worst in human behaviour. How can you love someone who might one day be capable of the very worst in human behaviour? How can you trust them, be kind to them, reassure them that they still have a place in this world, let alone talk them up and tell them that they are wonderful, unique and valuable and that the world would not be nearly as good a place without them?

The answer is, it's quite difficult actually.

Do I sound jaded? Perhaps I am. After all, I'm a middle-aged lawyer – both in birth years and in legal practice years, having been in practice for twenty years. I should be thoroughly burned out by now. I should stare down the long dusty corridor of the next twenty years of my legal career and cry out, 'Please someone, save me!' But somewhat bizarrely I'm one of the most content lawyers I know and for no other reason than the fact that I can honestly say I love who I am, what I do and I bloody love everything I stand for.

Let me be frank with you: this wasn't always the case. In fact, for the longest time my relationship with the Law resembled more a marriage of convenience than a love affair. My side of the bargain was that I would practise Law and in return I would get security and status – two things missing in my life and that represented to me the Holy Grail of happiness and fulfillment. But like most marriages of convenience, it has a rather limited lifespan.

Why?

Because you simply don't care enough. And when you don't care enough, a small part of you starts dying each day, day after day, until one day you wake up and find you are a shriveled husk of your former self. That's when you roll over and say, 'Law, I want a divorce'.

And the Law, having stopped caring about you a long time ago anyway, looks back at you, smirks and says, 'Well, go then! See if I care. You're nothing without me. I'm better off without you anyway.'

That's a Big Tears moment, the moment you and the Law threaten to part with one another forever. But it's a necessary part of the journey from a marriage of convenience to a – albeit later in life – love affair. But later-in-life love affairs are supposed to be the best love affairs anyway, aren't they?

At least, that's what I'm told.

But look, I hear you. You want to know why you, the reader, should care about my love affair with the Law? Well, it's simple really and it goes back to what I said at the start of this piece. It's hard enough to love yourself at the best of times, but if you're a lawyer, it's *real* hard. So if I can do it, anyone can.

Now let me tell you how it works.

Find Work that Has Meaning for You or Find Meaning in Your Work

Any kind of engagement you have that is motivated by external rewards and gains will eventually shrivel and die.

I don't really care what it is and I don't believe that there are any exceptions, so, seriously, don't waste your time looking for them. It might take a few years, it might take thirty but it (you) will break.

To avoid this you need to find a deeper meaning and value in what you do and you need to live a life that is congruent with that deeper meaning and value.

If there is too much of a disjunction between the two, you will suffer dis-ease. Dis-ease is a word that describes when you feel uneasy about yourself or your life and it manifests itself in physical and/or psychosomatic illness. It's a state of not being at ease with yourself, with others and with the world. It also feels like crap.

I may have started practising Law for all of the wrong reasons, but eventually I realised that it is my practise of Law that enables me to live out my deepest values.

I believe in the universal Law that all human beings are born equal, deserve love and protection, and have fundamental human rights that are worth safeguarding, whatever the cost. To me this universal Law is inalienable. It cannot be abrogated. Attempts are made, don't get me wrong, but to me this universal Law *is the natural order of things.*

My practise of the Law enables me to turn what I value most into real action each day of my life. I can't express enough how grateful I am that I can live out my deepest values rather than harbouring those values in my heart, but not being able to find expression for them. This puts me among the most privileged people in this world. What a luxury!

I am aware of this, which is why I say find meaning in your work or find work that has meaning for you.

I recognise that not everyone can choose their employment, but if you fit into this category then find ways to turn your engagement with work into meaning.

Even if this means donating some of what you earn to a charity that is meaningful to you, or even if it is as simple (*but as important*) as being able to provide nutritious food for your family, there will be a connection. Focus on that connection until you truly believe that what you do matters.

Find a Ritual for Honouring Your Deeper Meaning and Engage in it Regularly

I've never been one to meditate or utter mantras. It's just not in me. God knows I've tried the whole mindful meditation lifestyle and more than once too, but ... *nothing*.

I used to find this disheartening until I realised that I didn't actually need to meditate, utter mantras or engage in mindfulness exercises at all, because every single time I enter the courtroom I engage in a mindful practice. Every time I enter a courtroom, and every time I leave a courtroom, I bow. When I bow to the bench I am acknowledging that I am a small part of a system that is much bigger than me and to which I owe my allegiance.

These are not the only rituals I engage in either.

Even the language I use in the courtroom reminds me of my place. When I address the judge I call them 'Your Honour' and I always seek leave before approaching the judge's clerk or before I approach my client to get updated instructions. If I desperately need to go to the bathroom (called a convenience break) I beg the judicial officer's 'indulgence'. Some might find this language sycophantic but it is designed to act as a constant reminder that we are in service to the Law, not the other way around.

When lawyers are admitted to practice they have to take a vow that they will well and honestly demean themselves to the practice of the profession according to their best knowledge and ability. It's not every job that asks you to demean yourself now, is it? In this way you can see the vestiges of the clergy in our modern day legal system.

Early lawyers were almost always members of the clergy. Law was practised alongside religion and it was practised this way for an important reason – because Law was designed to capture the will of God and it's practise is a service to be engaged in.

Not much has changed. It just requires more thought and contemplation to see it this way and, once you do, even the most common rituals associated with the Law become meaningful and restorative. Sometimes you have to be creative.

Engage in the Ritual Practise of Reflection

I find this one easy as I have engaged in reflection as a way of living since I was a young child. My main method is to journal, which I do as a daily reflection.

Journaling helps me process the feelings I have associated with life and my work. It also acts as a record of my thoughts and perceptions. It's amazing how when you look back a year or two you can barely recognise yourself.

Why was I so angry about that?

Gee, I should have seen that coming for a mile!

Looking back regularly helps us contextualise what is happening to us today. It also has a humanising influence. When you are regularly and honestly recording everything that happens in your world you can't walk around imagining yourself to be a great deal better than everyone else. When you journal you quickly realise that over the course of your lifetime you've done all the dumb things too. Journaling is the great equaliser.

Journaling is not for everyone. Some people like to engage in therapeutic engagement with a professional. I have done this before and it was absolutely wonderful. The professional doesn't need to be a therapist; it can be a religious leader, or even a consultant in an area that impacts on your life.

One of the most valuable experiences I have ever had was through a paid mentorship that I was lucky enough to secure while working briefly in a government department. His name was John and he had this way of shrugging his shoulders.

'What if I end up a failure?'

(Shrugs his shoulders).

'What if I'm not suited to the Law?'

(Shrugs his shoulders).

'Do you think I have what it takes to see this career through?'

(Shrugs his shoulders).

Nice work if you can get it, huh?

But eventually I realised he was spot on. He was essentially saying to me that none of it really matters in the end, and he was right. He encouraged me to walk away from the Law if that was what I needed to do to re-find myself

Ironically, I did walk away (briefly) only to find that in the process of walking away, I fell in love with Law again, which leads me to the most important lesson.

Be Ready to Walk Away

This is essential. You have to walk away from a relationship when it turns bad and you feel unsafe in it.

If you're lucky, like I was, you walk away only to find that what was bad was just a combination of your misunderstandings of what was really required of you and the pressure of doing it well regardless. So you pick yourself up, recommit and find a way to be in it that is restorative, not threatening.

Not everyone is as lucky as me. One of my former mentors – a man who was deeply loved and respected by everyone he came across, and certainly every member of the legal community – recently took his own life.

He made sure he finished his day's work first, tidied his office and then drove down to a local quarry and hung himself.

The news of his death rocked the legal community. I couldn't work for weeks. I kept asking myself, *What does it take to bring such a good man down?* And, *If this wonderful man had reached the pinnacle of his career and was so widely loved and regarded but still took his own life, what does that mean for mere mortals like the rest of us?* And, *How can I be sure to keep myself safe in all of this?*

And then I remembered that he had once told me that he took a break from Law and spent months driving trucks. He said it was the happiest and the freest he had ever been.

I reflected on this after his death and I had to ask myself, *Why did he feel that he could not leave it all behind again? Why couldn't he just jump in a truck and drive down the highways he knew that would give him so much solace?*

I don't have the answers, but now when I think of him I try to think of him in a truck, laughing, wind in his hair, music blaring, loving life again. I worshipped that man.

What people often don't realise is that lawyers spend their lives amongst the broken and it hurts. It hurts to witness so much suffering and, at times, evil. When you're a young lawyer you tend to try to manage it all by shutting off your feelings. You feel like it's a bit of a superpower.

'Hey, I can hear all of these horrible stories and not feel anything!'

Nope! Delusional. It's a defense mechanism and it has a fairly short lifespan too. Want a sustainable career in Law? Learn to lean into the suffering. Had enough of the suffering? Walk away. Don't let anything in your life be more important than your health and wellbeing.

Lawyers are not the only people to work amongst the broken, obviously. But the same applies.

Sometimes, despite your best intentions and efforts, it all gets a bit too much and you need to listen to those warning signs and respect them. If you don't, you're not being true to yourself.

Your soul has an amazing capacity to speak to you, often through your own body.

Listen to it.

Find your Sanctuary
And for those who stay in it? Find your sanctuary.

Find it quickly.

Maybe you find sanctuary walking in the mountains or swimming in the ocean. Perhaps it's dance, driving, or having lovers. Maybe your sanctuary is in an artistic endeavor. I like to write stories about impossible places and unlikely characters.

Whatever it is, pursue it like someone with their hair on fire would pursue a pool of water.

It's never a waste of time or a meaningless endeavor to engage in activities that restore you to yourself.

When we find sanctuary we find a place to refuel, reflect and, if necessary, reassess.

Oh, and Hug a Lawyer Today
That's a joke. Sort of. Hug the people you know that need it most. Understand that everyone is suffering on some level. We can't read people's minds. We don't know what they are going through. I say 'hug lawyers' only because I am one and I know what it means to live with one. But hug anyone close to you, especially the ones you feel don't necessarily deserve it.

I specialise in child abuse cases. Sometimes I wake up in the middle of the night. You know how there is always a small period of time between sleep and full wakefulness? Well, in that time I have this incredibly disturbing dream.

I am walking around the streets at night. I have a torch in my hand and I keep shining the torch onto this house and then that house, but I can never find *the* house. Somewhere close by, I know a child is being abused, but what house was it again? They all look so similar. I stand and listen but I can't hear any sounds. Everyone seems to be sleeping peacefully so I turn to walk home again. As I'm walking back I know that she's out there but I have missed her. Again.

'It's okay ,' I tell myself. 'Tomorrow I'll find her. I'll find her tomorrow.'

Then I fall back asleep. When tomorrow comes, I get up, put on my suit and a bit of lippy and go to court.

'Today is the day I will find her,' I tell myself. 'Today is that day.'

Loving yourself begins and ends with loving others. When you love others, it is easy to love yourself. Even if you are a lawyer. Especially if you are a lawyer.

yoga teacher

The Spirit of Yoga

Kylie Hennessy

'You are joy, looking for a way to express. It's not just that your purpose is joy, it is that you are joy. You are love and joy and freedom and clarity expressing. Energy-frolicking and eager. That's who you are.'

— Abraham / Esther Hicks

Our Spirit is Potential

The ancient yogic traditions teach us of the innate wellness of our spirit within. Our spirit's nature is unbound joy, deep peace, and ever-expanding consciousness. Clarity of mind enables us to experience this in our daily life.

When we are completely absorbed in the present moment – such as beholding a beautiful sunset, looking into the eyes of a loved one, or listening to a baby laugh – we feel oneness, joy and peace. This is because our mind is in a state the yogis call *nirvichara samadhi*, which translates to absorption without conceptualisation of the mind.

> 'Nirvichara vaisharadyed atma prasad' (In the purity of nirvichara samadhi, the inner spirit shines.)
>
> – Sutra 1.47 The Yoga Sutras of Patanjali

We sense in our physical self our own true nature. We may call it names such as divine, the Goddess, God, source or self. Our spirit is never separate from the source of creation – or *prana* – that moves through us.

The enlightened but controversial Master Osho said, 'The flowering of our selves, our potential, is what makes our spirit's song heard, our hearts sing and our true self shines.'

In his commentary of the Ancient Buddhist Text, *The Dhammapada: the Way of the Buddha* (Vol 12, Ch 1), he says:

> 'A single seed is capable of making the whole earth green. It has so much potential – infinite potential, because out of a single seed millions of seeds will arise, and so on and so forth. If you have one single seed the whole earth can be a garden. Why just the whole earth? The whole universe can be a garden! The potential is infinite; you have just to find the right opportunity for its expression, for its manifestation, for its realisation.'

Modern science has arrived at the same understanding as in quantum physics: everything arises from the quantum field, which is pure potential and a void of things all at the same time.

> 'The atoms or elementary particles themselves are not real; they form a world of potentialities or possibilities rather than one of things or facts.'
>
> — Werner Heisenberg, pioneer in quantum mechanics

In quantum theory, it is said that the observer of matter alters the behaviour of the matter and everything is inseparable.

In splitting a photon of light (a photon being the smallest discrete amount or basic unit of all light) in two, it was found that even when separated at a distance in space when influencing one half in a certain way, it had the same effect on the other.

The experiences are sensed through our mind, body and breath and is influenced by our perception of the experiences.

When our mind is clouded with judgment, doubt or lack of clarity, our inner guidance system is harder to hear or feel.

Inner Wisdom

Our inner guidance system, our intuition, or what is also known as an inner husk, is always in harmony with our true nature. In Yoga it is referred to as our *Vijñāna* subtle body- *vi* – especially, *jnana* knowledge. Like water, it can take any shape or form, but the nature of it never changes. It knows where to go and what to do to create and fulfil our desires.

Our inner wisdom is in tune with the harmony of nature and what some may call the divine, or the universal truth. Impulses and intuition – especially in quieter states of mind/body – always feel joyful and give a sense of grace and connection to something greater.

This intuition is infinitely more intelligent than our psychological mind or personality mind. We receive thoughts of joy from this place of intuition, as opposed to the psychological/personality mind that analyses, worries and judges.

As we follow this inner knowing and our impulses, not only do we open ourselves to allowing the creative powers of the universe to deliberate as co-creators with the divine, but also with others around us that share the same desires to create and expand.

When these deep feelings of satisfaction pervade our life, we understand that it is an expansion of consciousness and that new exciting desires will manifest.

The Breath

> 'Breathing in, I calm body and mind. Breathing out, I smile. Dwelling in the present moment, I know this is the only moment.'
>
> – Thich Nhat Hanh

The most powerful way to quieten the outer mind and connect with our spirit is to focus on our breath. Regulating our breath steadies the mind and leads us to greater clarity and awareness.

If you pause for a few moments and take some time to steady your breath – breathing in and out slowly through the nose – can you sense your healthy spirit? When our mind and body are healthy, it is easier to accomplish.

However, if we shift our attention within – perhaps using our breath as a bridge to deeper levels of awareness – we can always access our healthy spirit.

In focusing our attention on beautiful or joyful life experiences, the inner sense of wellbeing grows. Many people find great peace and love when terminally ill, even though their body is unwell. Their focus shifts to their inner being's wellness.

> 'Prana, the vital breath, is born of Self, like a person and his shadow, the Self and the Prana are inseparable. Prana enters the body at birth, but does not die with the body.'
>
> – Prana Upanishads

Yogis and scientists alike have discovered that simple conscious-controlled nose breathing regulates all systems of the body. Our breath is what provides us with the life force and energy that keeps our spirit connected to our outer husk of the mind/body. When our breath is steady the mind/body is in a more balanced state, and thus we have more clarity and vitality, and our inner being shines.

Science now tells us that when we practise conscious-controlled nose breathing we release a cocktail of chemical messengers – feel good hormones known as the 'molecules of emotions'.

> 'Emotions are the nexus between matter and mind, going back and forth between the two and influencing both.'
>
> — Candace B. Pert

Some of these released hormones are oxytocin and endorphins. Oxytocin – known as an anti-anxiety hormone – is the hormone of calmness, love and connection, and it also relieves pain. Endorphins are the hormone of transcendence, a powerful opiate and pain-relieving substance, which gives us a sense of wellbeing and feeling present in the moment. This brings us into more harmony with our inner spirit.

Deep breathing also activates the biological state researched by Dr Herbert Benson – author of *The Relaxation Response* – in which our mind calms down, our heartrate slows, and we switch on the parasympathetic nervous system.

Dr Andrew Weil, an integrative doctor and researcher, has noted in his work that 'there is something spiritual about breathwork' which connects us beyond the mind. He points out that in many languages, the word for 'breath' has roots back to the word 'spirit'. The Latin word for breath, *spiritus*, has connections to 'spirit' and 'inspire'. When we feel that connection to spirit we are inspired and guided through life through wisdom, *vijnana* (special knowledge), as is described in the ancient Vedic texts.

Our Spirit's Satisfaction with Allowing Creation to Flow

We feel our healthy spirit when we are experiencing and expressing our true selves through our senses of our body/mind.

If our experience can be of less fear and suffering of the mind, then our inner being is never in a state of suffering.

Our spirit knows that all experiences of contrast in our human physical experience is a part of the natural rhythm of life, which causes us to know what we want and don't want. We can allow a sense of creativity and joy to flow.

The Cycles of Creation

> 'You didn't come for the manifestation ... you came for the manifesting. You didn't come for the creation ... you came for the creating. You came because you are a Creator and a Creator's gotta create.'
>
> — Abraham / Esther Hicks

Just like the laws of nature, there is no light without dark, there is no winter without summer, yin is only relational to yang and neither exist without each other. With each death there is a birth and with each birth there is a death.

Research done by scientists at the HeartMath Institute have confirmed when we are in positive emotional states – such as joy, compassion and care – our heart emits electromagnetic forces which bring harmony to our body/mind/breath physiologically and energetically.

The heart sends more messages to the brain than the brain sends to the heart and these electromagnetic fields, produced by the human heart, extend into our physical world and beyond our body.

In fact, scientist have found that the human heart is the strongest generator of the electrical and magnetic forces in our body and increases its electromagnetic radiation when we are in positive states of emotion.

At a quantum level, it is electrical and magnetic radiation that cause atoms and molecules to rearrange and change characteristics, which we then see as a change in the physical world. Scientist Gregg Braden confirms this power of our mind to create our physical reality.

This all begins with an experience that causes us to think about something we want and then feeling in our heart what it would be like to have it.

When we contemplate this with a sense of joy and gratitude, for example, the heart amplifies the output of electromagnetic radiation (up to 60 times more electrical and 5000 times more magnetically, according the Heart Math Institute research) causing a change in our physical reality.

When we begin *feeling* what we want to create in our lives, those feelings then create the electromagnetic patterns which are like a template for electromagnetic radiations. In these states it has also been found we can process information very quickly and can access extraordinary states of intuition.

When we are in alignment with our true nature and feeling more inner joy, we can access more creative power within and influence our reality using the power of mind and heart. With this, our healthy spirit shines and blossoms into our ever-expanding potential.

Shakti Energy – Allowing the Energy of Creation to Flow

The chakras – or energy centres of the body – can be a tool to understanding ourselves. They can be used to become more deliberate creators in our life and tune back into our spirit within.

From the crown to the base, our energy centres are aligned along a central channel of energy called the *sushumna*, which allows the energy to flow between spirit and matter. The highest chakra, at the crown of the head, has the highest energetic vibration and is more connected to spirit. The lowest chakra at the base of our spine, has the lowest vibration of energy, and it relates to our physical self and our world of matter. The crown chakra is where we connect to our higher self and our inspired ideas and desires. The crown chakra is represented as the 1000 petal lotus flower in bloom.

The third eye is the centre of our imagination and intuition. It helps us to see these things more clearly and once we see clear visions of things we want to be, do, or have, we then receive the inner guidance to create.

The throat chakra holds our belief systems and is where we express our inner truths. It also gives us power to speak about what we want. When we believe we can have what we want, and it is aligned with our heart's desire, the magic begins to unfold.

The heart is where we have our 'wishing tree'. Spending time in prayer or feeling appreciation in the heart by believing, seeing and feeling our desire as if already present, amplifies the electromagnetic fields the heart emits. When the outer mind is quiet, we can focus solely on what we want. The heart does not judge, it does not doubt, it does not worry. It is said in yoga, and many ancient cultures, to be the seat of our soul.

The third chakra is our centre of personal will. It's where the ego acts. It trusts and listens to divine timing. Listen to this inner wisdom with joy and passion as its guidance system. We have a masculine aspect of the power centre, the solar plexus, which uses the power of action. We also have a feminine aspect, the lunar plexus, which knows the power of patience and reflection.

As the energy of this idea moves into the belly, or the sacral chakra, our centre of creativity, desire and sensuality, we begin to feel a sense of co-creating in the physical world. The dance of creation begins to show physical, more tangible signs. Relationships with others, or things in nature, start to reveal the pieces of our inspiration coming together.

Our base chakra has the lowest and slowest vibrations of energy and turns our thoughts to matter. We start walking this truth and living it in our physical experience, as is the full manifestation that takes place.

By doing simple meditations or visualisations of the things we want to create starting with the crown chakra and moving down through each chakra to the base we can clarify our vision and beliefs. This helps our mind and body move into the expansion of spirit.

Opportunity for Expansion

Consider the term disease for a moment, *dis-ease* ... a lack of ease. B.K.S. Iyengar said, 'Yoga can cure that which can be cured and help us endure that which cannot.' We can use feelings of dis-ease as an indicator to listen internally to what will bring us back into ease. Releasing tension brings us back into ease.

The yoga *asana*, or postures, help us quiet the mind and release tension in the subconscious mind. This helps us to practise living in a state of comfort, stability and ease, which is the very nature of a healthy spirit.

Our *pranayama* and simple breathing practices also help to quiet the mind and connect us to our inner spirit: the inhalation taking in life and the exhalation letting things go. This will allow for the next moment or experience to come and allow our body and mind to move with the expanded consciousness. It certainly doesn't have to be complicated or take years of spiritual discipline to potentially become enlightened.

As we 'follow our bliss', as Joseph Campbell guided us, we can realise our healthy spirit within our everyday moments of life. If that takes us to a yoga mat, great. If it takes us to the ocean or takes us to spending time with family or friends, perfect! Let your inner joy guide you.

It's much simpler than the mind may think.

trauma counsellor

Beannacht:
The Spiritual Care of Irish Blessing

Mary Jo Mc Veigh

Dedicated to Clare Mc Veigh

The great divine brought us together in the sacred contract of mother and daughter. An eternal, unbreakable connection of love.

Le grá mór

I would like to acknowledge the traditional guardian of the land (Sydney) upon which this chapter was written. Pay my respects to and honour the wisdom of the elders, past, present and future. I recognise the dignity, vibrancy and strength of the culture they hold true.

A blessing to read this chapter by:

May you be in the sacred company of these words,

May these words bring comfort to your heart and healing to your spirit,

May you find in them, a cadence to journey by,

May your travels be for the health of your spirit.

Introduction

Do you care for your spirit as you care for your body?
I have often asked this question. It sometimes receives a 'yes'; more often a shrug; and, mostly, a resounding 'no'. People who respond in the affirmative, and describe themselves as religious, speak about praying or going to religious services. People who identify with being spiritual outside religion often name meditation or visualisation as their practice.

In a society where the corporal construction of the self exists in a materialistic world, attendance to physical care is often more prevalent than the spiritual care. Cleaning and clothing the body, exercising, and eating nutritious food as practices of care for the body are more easily recognised. Care of the spirit is not so commonly accepted as a daily routine.

I would like to focus on one aspect of Celtic Irish spirituality: Beannacht (blessing). As I share my experience of the gifts of Beannacht, I will pause in writing and create a space for your Beannacht to rise from within you. I will interchange the use of the words Beannacht and blessing to honour my ancestral language and recognise you as a reader of the English language.

> When I embraced the gifts of blessings I bought myself a journal. It has now turned into journals. I can write one word, a line, an entire blessing in one sitting. So, before reading on, buy yourself a journal and as the thoughts arise when reading put an entry into your journal.

Tribute to John O'Donohue

John O'Donohue was the catalyst for me to find the courage to re-engage in seeking spiritual care from the wisdom of my own people. His literary works have been scattered throughout twenty-five years of my life as much as they have been scattered over the coffee tables, floors and bedside cabinets upon which they rested after I read and reread them.

Death took John in 2008 to walk in the spiritual realm of our ancestors. His parting left the world bereft of the beauty of his being and spiritual wisdom, yet as John Quinn (2015, p.17) reminds us, 'In the years since he left us, John's presence is more vivid and pure than ever in the lives of many.'

Thank you, John. I hope I honour your work in this chapter by keeping the blessed fire of Celtic knowledge burning to warm the spirits of all travellers who seek comfort in its heat.

Finding My Definition

Beannacht as a written or spoken form is a sacred bridge that connects me to the divine. I tread as WB Yeats invites me to, 'softly', not on dreams, but on the sacred structure of the blessing.

When I bless, I am traversing the physicality of my heart and cognitions of my mind to be with the divine. Although the ancient Celts honoured the integration of the spiritual in everyday life, they still felt it was important to purposefully call upon the sacred or name the sacred. A Beannacht as a ritual of words honours this and as John O' Donohue (2007, p.14) reminds us, 'evokes a sense or warmth and protection; it suggests that no life is alone or unreachable.'

John O' Donohue (2001, p.201) writes of the labour of blessing that 'when we bless, we work from a place of inner vision, clearer than our hearts, brighter than our minds.' In the spirituality charged life of the Irish the finished words of the Beannacht is the blessing, the labour of the Beannacht is the blessing, the energy transfer from the person creating the blessing to the words is the blessing. Beannacht is a sacred matrix of life, a sacred pattern that connects us all.

> Write what the word blessing means to you.
> Or
> Write an invocation to invite blessing into your life.
> Or
> Write down any thoughts that arise upon reading this definition section.

There is No Right Way, Just 'The Sacred Way'
When I studied English at school, I was taught that there was a right and a wrong. We were instructed on correct punctuation, grammatical rules and standards of essay writing. The creation of a written or spoken Beannacht does not have rules. The spiritual emphasis is to connect with the divine and to live through the divine.

I will offer some pointers that can guide you in the creation of your blessings, but spiritual health in the Beannacht is contained in listening to yourself and the divine all around you. The person offering Beannacht can invoke the gifts of the natural elements for themselves or others, use the potential for healing within the formation of words, engage in acts of offering, and celebrate the noticed moments of life.

Every moment in life is an opening for the ritual of Beannacht to occur.

The Forms of the Beannacht

The rhythmic form of Beannacht is important. The cadenced use of language is a calling forth. It is an invocation of pulsing words that will strengthen the link between you and the sacred.

The relational spirituality of the Celtic Irish is carried on the creation of the Beannacht and based upon the Irish language is often written as a relational exchange. Therefore, when writing a Beannacht for someone the phrases, ' to you', 'upon you', and 'with you' are used.

The most commonly known form of this is the use of the word 'May', hence lines like , 'May you always feel the warmth of the sun rest upon your face'.

Other cadenced forms are the repetitive use of word or description. For example, 'Deep peace of the gentle rain to you. Deep peace of the soft light to you.'

Beannacht also uses any form of poetic stanzas with language laden with rich descriptions that defy seemingly factual reality. The following is an extract from a blessing I wrote when I was healing from a time of illness:

'May your body be a blessed library of wisdom to you.

May you read deep into its wisdom and find healing there.'

It is obvious that the physical body does not contain books that would allow it to be described as a library, as is the dictionary definition, but to the creative mind of the soul it is a reading room to sit in, read what is there and gain wisdom that can be used in the care of the spirit.

> Use repetition to write a Beannacht. Start each sentence with the same phrase, for example, 'Healing warmth of the sun to you. Healing cool of the water to you ...'

Nature-Based Blessing
In our belief in the spiritual identity of all life and elements in the cosmos we acknowledge that there is wisdom to be called upon within them. The universe is abundant with wisdom: trees speak in the rustle of their leaves, clarity comes in the brightness of the sun, and cleansing comes in the flowing of a river.

Think of the geological age of mountains and the solid presence of their mass. Being present for many years, watching what unfolds season after season without interfering, allows for an outlook on life that is steeped in the knowledge of being present.

Humans cannot reach this longevity, but we can attach our thinking to the mountain and listen to what the spirit of the mountain can teach us.

Several years ago, I went to Peru to walk the Inca trail to Machu Picchu as part of my healing from a great trauma. Looking back, I see myself walking that ancient path and feel the ache in my heart, the tightness in my muscles, and the tinge of despair when I look to the pinnacle, overwhelmed by the distance. I feel the irritation of looking down at my feet because I cannot see the path ahead of me.

And then comes the moment of a choice that propels me forward.

I place my eyes on the mountain path and to what feels comfortable in achieving. I shift my gaze to my range of comfort, and my eyes reawaken to the beauty of the mountain. I see native orchids, sunlight playing chase and catch with ripples in the small stream by my side, a humming bird flying by and saying hello.

The discovery of this beauty fuels my spirit and energises me. The drudgery of the walk disappears. I send questions out. Does the mountain know that in my time of despair I need encouragement? And does it know to place the signs of beauty right at the level of my sight to keep me going? From the annals of my Celtic Irish spirituality the answer is YES.

I blessed that mountain on that day, a blessing of deep love and gratitude. Moreover, in the years since, when I face a seemingly insurmountable problem I turn my spiritual attention to the mountains and ask for their wisdom again.

The Celtic spirituality and union with nature is integrated throughout an Irish way of life. In everyone's birth story (dependent on the time of year you were born) there is a bestowing of the power of a tree or plant and the protection or quality of an animal. Even our ancient alphabet – called the Ogham – was nature based. It was known as the Celtic tree alphabet as each letter represented a tree or plant.

Animal or plant based Beannacht is therefore a powerful invocation. It holds the mystical powers of the life forms it venerates. It is one of my favourite ways of sacred connection. It serves me well for many different purposes.

I have often used nature invocations in many ways, e.g. to replenish my personal energy source when it is draining, when I want to celebrate, show gratitude to life or write for someone else. The abundance of the wisdom of nature means that it can be used for many purposes and does not deplete when it is called upon.

> Choose a place in nature, an elemental feature, a plant or animal. Write down it's characteristics or any wisdom it speaks to you. Write a blessing using the cadence of the Irish blessing format of 'May the'

Significant Sacred Place

Everyone can connect to this divine energy source, but the more you are attuned to the spiritual nature of life the more you feel it when you are in its presence. While I have had multiple experiences of 'plugging in' in different countries, there is nothing like going home to Ireland. It is like super-charging my soul battery.

However, it does not take a return to my country of birth to spiritually recharge. When you accept that Spirit is all around, then it is all around. And while urbanisation may mute the natural force of the land, water and air, it is still there. I encourage people to create a place of sacred significance in their own homes.

This place does not have to be large – just big enough for a table and a chair. Place upon it any images that represent your connection to spiritual identity. Artefacts of nature are paramount – flowers or herbs from your garden, a feather found on the street, a beautiful dried leaf retrieved from the gutter. It is like nature dropping little prayers in the cemented maze of city streets.

> For those readers who do not have a significantly sacred place in their home, stop reading and plan one. Choose a place in your home away from a television or other large electrical equipment. Think about what you would like to place on it, and now go and do it.

Relational Blessing

In the Irish spoken tongue, greetings were relational. We acknowledged the divine within each other. This divinity greeting was *Dia Duit* and the response was *Dia is Muire duit*. Which translate to, 'God be with you', 'Mary and God be with you.' In pre-Christian Ireland the greeting was not referring to a Christian god. It was the recognition of the spiritual within and all around each of us.

The response which includes Mary is significant. The Celtic Irish love of Earth as mother was strong. The modern Irish name for Ireland, Éire, comes from the ancient name for Ireland, Éiru. Éiru was a name of a Celtic Goddess, matron sovereign of the land. So, in response to a person greeting that acknowledged the divine in you, the returned acknowledgment also included recognising the divinity of the land. With Christianity came the reverence of Mary, the mother of Christ, and hence Mary took the place of the Goddess.

This relational spirituality found in our ancient greeting runs throughout the core of all blessings. The words of the blessings built a relationship. For example, the author of the Beannacht may use the gifts of nature or animals and in this act of recognition personally connect to them and pass the essence of the animal of plant to the receiver of the blessing. The sending of the blessing continues this interpersonal undertaking. The words bind the giver and the receiver in a sacred contract that fulfils what the content of the blessing is intended for, e.g., if you send a blessing to someone when they are sick, even if you are not with them physically, the words of the blessing connect you through distance and for the duration of the sickness. In this instance you might create something like:

Renewal of the new sun to you,

Balm of the morning dew to you,

Calm of the still water to you,

Healing of the silent forest to you.

Bring someone to mind and write a blessing for them. Use the elements and bounties of nature. Finish each line of the blessing with 'to you'.

Hard Times of Life

A dear friend of mine was going through a hard time. Some gave her advice, some cajoled her, and others ignored her problems all together. She spoke of this time as, 'Everything has gone to shit.' So I wrote her a Beannacht as an act of my love and unremitting presence in her life.

One verse included the following:

> *With all the shit and glory that life has brought your way,*
>
> *You have the chance to start afresh each and every day.*
>
> *From all the shit and glory that life has brought your way,*
>
> *You have the chance to make your mark and not stay silent in your say.*
>
> *Alongside all the shit and glory that life has brought your way,*
>
> *There is some hope and happiness when you are ready for the stay.*

Some seasonal elements can seem unforgiving – storms, fires, blizzards, the scorching winds – but they are all loved by the spiritual creator and all have a sacred contract with the land. It is with the elements of human experiences that a strong Beannacht is often called for.

> Think of a difficult time in your own life or the life of someone you love. Grab some strong words to describe this time and list them. When your list is complete write a list that is the opposite to each of these words.
> Settle yourself in quiet calmness for a moment. Now weave the two list of words together in sentences to create a Beannacht to the difficult time.

The Spiritual Lorica

The Celts believed that it was important to wear a Lorica – the anglicised version of Lorica is breastplate – when facing spiritually dangerous times. The power of the Lorica Beannacht lies in the words that are woven together to create as comprehensive a shield as possible. In Christian Ireland the most renowned and often quoted Lorica is attributed to St Patrick, though some scholars believe the author is anonymous.

Many years ago, I was working with a young boy plagued by nightmares and tortured by a school bully. The boy revealed his love of medieval knights and his aunty, who was an angel in his life. As he talked about these two loves I could hear words arising from within the internal landscape of my mind to fill the space between us

I said, 'What you need is a breastplate like ...'

Angels be with me, angels within me,

Angels behind me, angels before me,

Angels beside me, angels to win me,

Angels to comfort me and restore me.

Angels beneath me, angels above me,

Angels in quiet, angels in danger,

Angels in hearts of all that love me,

Angels in mouth of friend and stranger.

Unplanned, I had taken a verse from the breastplate of St Patrick and replaced the word 'Christ' with 'Angel' to resonate with his love of his angelic aunt, and to link it with his love of mediaeval knights. We then took a large piece of cardboard and drew a shield on it. Upon this shield he drew pictures that represented protection, love, strength and I wrote him out the angelic verse.

The therapeutic power of this shield for this boy was pivotal in the creation of a healing program I wrote for children and young people (Mc Veigh, 2006). Moreover, it reminded me of the importance of including the Lorica in my Beannacht practices.

> Using the angel verse above, write your own Lorica by replacing the word angel with another word, for example, 'Love be with me, love within me, love behind me and before me ...'

Sassy Spirituality

Being in the presence of human suffering in a professional capacity for over thirty years has not dulled my sense of fun, attraction to the ridiculous, or my ability to laugh louder than most (to the dismay of my sons, who now refuse to go to the movies with me).

Joy is a sacred gift, so my love of fun has come into my spiritual practices with what I call the sassy Beannacht. These are blessings that allow us to giggle and delight at the world or poke a bit of loving fun at ourselves or dwell in the ridiculous just for a moment before we feel the weight of life's burdens again. For me, laughter is the work of the angels.

I have written several sassy and silly blessings, especially for children. In doing so, I have not only brought myself joy in writing, but watched the glee on people's faces as I have read them. Our collective joy flows and our connection to the presence of the divine deepens.

At the end of my training course I recited one of my favourite Beannachts by John O' Donohue (2007). I recite this at the end of many of my training courses as a gift of recognition to my professional colleagues and to bless the work they do.

The first two stanzas are:

> *On the day when the weight deadens*
>
> *on your shoulders and you stumble,*
>
> *may the clay dance to balance you.*
>
> *And when your eyes freeze behind the grey window*
>
> *and the ghost of loss gets into you,*
>
> *may a flock of colours,*
>
> *indigo, red, green and azure blue*
>
> *come to awaken in you a meadow of delight.*

Several years ago, after one of my courses, I received an email from one of the of the participants. He had taken John's words and wrote what he termed an Australian version. I laughed heartedly as I read it. It took iconic Australia into the land of Beannacht with precision and humour and is a prime example of a sassy Beannacht.

I had intended to send it to John; he would have loved reading it. Sadly, he died shortly after I received it. Perhaps he can read it now and still send us out his laughter.

The Australian version:

On the day when the weight cuts into
your sunburn and you stumble
May the bindi eyes dance to be your thongs.
And when your eyes freeze behind the tinted sunnies
and the upturned esky of loss gets into you,
May a flock of gallahs,
indigo, red, green and azure blue,
Come to awaken in you a mambo shirt of delight.

> Think of something fun you do in your life or think of a cheeky moment, take the activity or moment and turn it into your sassy blessing.

Blessing the Ordinary

Like my Celtic ancestors I do not believe that 'God' resides in some distant kingdom or that spiritual wisdom belongs only to a chosen few. I hold firm to our ancient beliefs that the sacred is all around me – from the tiny leaf to the large standing stones in a rocky outcrop.

When my children were young they loved to call for attention with, 'Mama, Mama, come look,' or, 'Mama, Mama, watch me,' or, 'Again, Mama, again!' It was a constant call from the rise of morning to the dark of the day, and sometimes beyond if they had nightmares. I dared not pick up a phone to call a friend because as soon as I had three digits dialled, the domestic anthem of 'Mama ...' would begin. Running a warm relaxing bath when they were awake was a no-no and planning to get to the toilet without a babbling conversation ensuing from the other side of the door took military stealth. But when I went to the washing line ... stillness. It worked every time. I attached a laundry basket to my hip and the 'Mama' calls seemed to disappear.

A few years ago, as I was hanging out the washing I noticed the silence. But this time it was because of their absence. They are young men now, living full independent lives. The memory of them young rolled down my cheek as a tear. I looked at my tear-stained memory and saw many happy times when they were little boys. I stood in the garden in that ordinary laundry basket moment and allowed a Beannacht to rise.

Blessing by the washing line.

Go raibh maith agat[1] for the clothes that I hang here today.

Go raibh maith agat for the means to buy these clothes.

---
1. Irish for thank you

Go raibh maith agat for the physical ability of this labour.

Go raibh maith agat for the freedom to engage in this most ordinary of acts.

Go raibh maith agat for the love of hanging the clothes of the past .

I realised many years ago that the seemingly ordinary may be a long-sought thing for another person. This realisation came on a yoga mat. My frustration at my lack of dexterity was multiplied by the vision of several wonderful human pretzels around me. Self-deprecation was added to my frustration and the yoga pose eluded me even further.

At the pinnacle of my disappointment, grace stepped forward. I was invited to think about all the people whose bodies were wrecked with pain or sickness or immobility. What would they give to have just one moment on this mat being as imperfect as me? I had lost touch with the blessed physical life I live. My vision of the gift of movement changed and I blessed my body. In that moment, with incredible ease, the posture was achieved.

There is NO ORDINARY in life.

It is all blessed.

> Pick a task you do which you feel is mundane, or routine. Think of the benefits of the task or someone associated with this task. Write your Beannacht of acknowledgment and watch how your words lift you out of the ordinary.

Connecting With All

Several years ago, I had to spend a day fasting and drinking a pre-surgery liquid to cleanse my system.

Towards the end of the day I felt hungry, drained and I dreaded the thought of gulping down more of the foul-tasting liquid.

I can see myself standing in my bedroom, tears welling in my eyes, unable to move my legs to the kitchen to drink once more.

When I felt my hunger, the sacred thought arose. My hunger was a signal of my survival. I was given the opportunity to have an operation that would save my life.

In that realisation I felt the hunger of my people in famine. There, hunger was a signal of their death.

My self-focus became them-focused, an experience of sacred belonging. I fell out of my own experience and fell in love with humanity.

I wrote:

> *Blessed is the hunger that lives.*
> *Blessed is the hunger that dies.*
> *Blessed is our suffering with each other.*
> *Blessed is our suffering for each other.*
> *Blessed is our love.*
> *Blessed is our love.*
> *Blessed is our love.*

> Think of a time of your suffering. Take this experience and connect it to others through your words.

Celebrating

Recognising our connection through human suffering also calls for a recognition of a celebratory life. This wards off falling into despair.

Life is full of ample opportunities to celebrate: the birth of a child, achievements of any kind, anniversaries of significance, the list goes on.

All these are great occasions to write a blessing and for those of you who are multi-talented you could even put your words to music.

> Think of something you want to celebrate and write a blessing.

The Blessing that Waits for You

As you live your life more from the realm of the sacred, you will see that the divine will find you without you having to go and look for it. Beannacht will rise from all around you.

I was sitting in the hairdressers one day. It seemed like any other appointment: colour, cut, blow dry. I sipped tea, absorbing the orchestral sound of the whirr of the hairdryer, the splash of the water and the hiss of the hair spray when I heard the words of a Beannacht rise:

I heard someone pray today and no-one seemed to care.

Even when their worship soared far into the air.

Perhaps this prayer remained unnoticed because of its humble grace.

For it did not rise in church, or cathedral.

But in the daily work of this place.

The Beannacht that comes cannot be forced. Do not analyse or overthink it. Be with it and, as soon as you can, write it down.

I sometimes sit in silence to be in the presence of the spiritual all around. Some days the Beannacht rises clearly above the din of my mind and puts words to the sacred message, and on other days I do not hear words but I hear the sacred noises of life: the noise of a passing train reminding me I have the gift of hearing, the light touch of a cool winter morning telling me I have the gift of life in my body, the movement of my fingers over the keyboard showing me I have sight to see the glorious wonders of this world.

> Place down your book after reading this invitation to be still.
>
> And just wait for the Beannacht that comes to you, either in your mind or the noises and sight of the life around you.

In Parting

The more I take the Beannacht journey, the more familiar the path becomes, the more its familiarity brings me comfort, keeps me connected and helps keep me healthy in spirit.

And so my parting words to you: when taking the spiritual path bring with you the ritual of Beannacht. Integrate it into your daily self-care regime to maintain your spiritual health.

My final Beannacht to you:

As you write the chapters of your own life,

May you call upon the wisdom of the sacred belonging.

May this calling,

invoke the strength of the land,

the company of your many brother and sisters,

the eternal love of your ancestors.

As you write the chapters of your life,

May you call upon the wisdom of the sacred belonging.

References

Coulter, S. (2014). (Re)Introducing themes of religion and spirituality to professional social work training in the land of 'Saints and Scholars', in C.E. Readdick (Ed.),*Groves Monographs on Marriage and Family. Volume 3: Irish Families and Globalization: Conversations about Belonging and Identity across Space and Time.* (pp. 1227–1242). Michigan: Michigan Publishing.

Mc Veigh, M.J. (2006). *Wrapped in Angels.* Sydney: Cara Counselling and Consultancy.

Mc Veigh, M.J. (2015).Sacred Harmony, in *Healthy Mind.* Eltham Victoria: Busybird Publishing.

O'Donohue, N.D. (2001). *The Angels Keep their Ancient Places. Reflection on Celtic Spirituality.* Edinburgh & New York: T & T Clark.

O'Donohue, J. (2007). *Benedictus. A Book of Blessings.* London: Bantam Press.

counsellor

The Long Way Home

Eric Hudson

> *Oh Nobly Born,*
> *Remember the pure open sky of your own true nature:*
> *Return to it.*
> *Trust it.*
> *It is home.*
> *– The words of the Buddha*

When I first read these words attributed to the Buddha, I felt a resonance with the notion of my own true nature of 'home' – a place to be trusted, a place of safety in this world. To be called back to a sense of my own true nature, something as pure as the open sky, stirred me. This is the most meaningful way for me to capture and to try to describe my spiritual journey.

It was several years ago now – my fortieth birthday – that I travelled to the mountains with my wife, and chose a painting to celebrate the occasion. The painting called to me – something about it was reminiscent of my childhood visits to my paternal grandparents' humble home on the outskirts of the mountain village where they lived.

Different to the traditional mountain vistas of other artists that featured sharp escarpments and deep valleys, this one avoided the popular cliché images. In dusty pinks, beautiful wispy clouded skies, and subtle greens of vegetation, two children wandered along a sandy bush track. Ahead, a patient parent waited. Behind the tops of trees, chimney smoke from a hidden house sent out a warm message of safety.

It was only after we made the purchase that I turned the painting over and discovered the name ascribed by the artist: 'The Long Way Home.' This encapsulated my experience, and continues to do so.

Five years earlier a process of deep change had been birthed in me. Dark secrets that had been held for more than twenty-five years had begun to open up. I began to speak. It was almost accidental. My childhood trauma bubbled out.

Through gut-wrenching sobs, as I spoke about my father's premature death, a deep crevasse of grief opened up. I realised a profound connection for the first time: my father discovered that I was being sexually abused, and now he was gone, he was no longer there to talk with.

Until that time no one else knew – just my abuser and myself. It was my father who found him with me in a bedroom. I was thirteen. The abuse started more than a year earlier. I was face down on the bed with the abuser – a young man – on top of me. It ended quickly, the abuser leaving the house, my father calling me outside to ask me, 'What were you doing?'

I had no answer.

We didn't speak about it again. This was a conversation that I would never have, but always wanted to.

I realised many years later that my father acted swiftly and decisively, ensuring that this man would never touch me again.

My father protected me.

***

As I reflect now I wonder about the mixing of different forces in my life. My maternal grandmother, a gracious godly woman made sure I owned a Bible, gave me Jesus storybooks as a child, and encouraged us to attend Sunday School. Jesus was alluring – he did and said amazing things that captured my attention. I took seriously my learning about him and the teaching of the church.

In the face of the guilty, shameful secrets I carried, I followed a path that somehow made everything bearable. I needed to be okay. I was a boy, afraid of being gay, of not being fully a man, and not fitting as a man in the world.

So I adopted this path of being good, compliant, a helper, not getting into trouble, and creating the best impression possible. Doing the right thing became a way of life. Along with this pattern I carried a deep-seated mix of guilt, shame and fear. I was afraid of what the abuse meant about me. I felt bad that somehow it was my fault, that I was to blame. I felt the stain of a dirty secret. I also discovered only very recently that my body naturally learned to hold itself in a tense, alert, defensive state. I was never really comfortable and relaxed.

As I began in my mid-thirties to reconcile being sexually assaulted as a 12- to 13-year-old boy, another truth slowly became evident: at the time I was being abused, I remember hearing the word 'poofter'. I asked what it meant. What I heard was a description of what was being done to me. I couldn't be like my abuser and hurt others like he was hurting me. I had to keep quiet. No one could find out. I was also confused.

Unconsciously, I set about to prove I was okay, normal, a man, a good man. And part of being good was connected to being religious. Being a part of a church where following Jesus felt normal and acceptable was a place to belong. And perhaps also a place to hide.

In the midst of the emerging AIDS crisis, the realisation of my same-sex attraction was dawning inside me. But I was married, with four young children and holding down a responsible position in my local church. This could not be true. This *must* not be true. Another layer of guilt and fear and shame was evident.

I had always felt different as a child to my three brothers. I was interested in different things. I liked different games. I didn't feel as though I belonged or fitted into the world of men and boys. I felt weak, inadequate, not good enough. I thought of myself as soft and 'girly'.

In fact, others often – yes, I mean *often* – told me I 'should have been a girl'. My world had no role models for me. The handsome male movie stars whose photos I pasted on my bedroom walls held their own secrets. I was growing up as a gay boy but I didn't know it. And because I didn't know it, I did the normal things that boys did, like having a girlfriend, getting married, becoming a father. And I was good at it. I had a good job, a responsible career, was an active and involved dad and a loving, supportive husband, all of the time pursuing my Christian faith.

All of the time covering my dark and shameful secret.

It would be a long time before I would voice the truth about being gay. And when I did, it was the catalyst for a long and painful journey for my wife and me. There is too much to say about that journey here, but enough to say that I realise that my journey of spirituality is inextricably entwined with the reality of my life journey: who am I, what is my purpose and passion, and how do I live truthfully and authentically. It seems odd to talk about living truthfully when I lived for so long with two interdependent secrets.

There was another contradiction.

I trained to be a relationship counsellor. And I was good at it. I enjoyed it. There was a convergence of my skills and experience, and it felt like a life calling. Being present with other people in the crises of their lives was both satisfying and challenging. This was a sacred space for me. I was confronting myself and my own truth at the same time. Internally I was moving through a long and gradual process that meant that I began to accept my own reality instead of denying, ignoring and repressing it. It was a long way home, a long way home to me, to myself.

My early religious frame of reference focused on sin, repentance and salvation. This lens magnified the feelings of guilt and shame that had been building. I sometimes wonder what my life would have been like and what it would be like now if the idea or notion of 'sin' did not exist.

One thing it would mean is that I would look at life through a different lens. Being a victim of child sexual assault would not need to be hidden in guilt and shame. Having sexual desires and acting on them would not need to be confessed. Being gay would not need to be hidden. The notion of sin limits the splendour and grace of being human. This is what is central for me: being human and being fully alive. This is the centre of my spirituality. It means accepting my humanity, celebrating my human experience, and not limiting my connections due to old self-images.

I am drawn to Aboriginal spirituality that sees Spirit dwelling in every part of the natural world. The Pitjantjatjara word *kanyini* speaks of the connections between spirit, country and land, lore, family and kin. It is a principle of unconditional love and responsibility for all things. It speaks to me of wholeness and integration, of compassion and authenticity.

I have a Celtic tattoo on my left arm, with four interconnected parts, representing my physical self, my mental self, my emotional self and my erotic self. Their connection and integration symbolises my spiritual self. A small gap between each quadrant symbolises a reaching out in all directions with my life purpose, to love and to bring love.

It is now some years since I visited Nepal and parts of northern India. I was already disenchanted with the hierarchies and abuses of power that I had been encountering within the church structures. I came away from that trip with a resolution to disconnect myself from any further structural and institutional expressions of faith and spirituality.

My connection with spirit and soul would be a much more individual journey.

I do not always get it right. Sometimes I am unhappy with the way I respond to other people. Sometimes my observations turn into judgements or assumptions. Sometimes I say and do things, or make decisions that hurt others.

Even though I don't always get it right, my heart intention is to live with kindness and integrity, authenticity and compassion, to be 'in the moment' as much as possible.

My life purpose – to love and to bring love – is a grounding energy that guides my path. I draw from a number of spiritual disciplines that resonate with me and that fit for me.

I am drawn to the pursuit of kindness as a useful guide in my life. When I greet a friend or acquaintance who is comfortable receiving an extended hug, I share four breaths with that person in the hug.

With each breath I internally recite the Buddhist prayer:

May I be kind (to you)

May I be loving (to you)

May I be compassionate (to you)

May I be at peace (with you.)

This prayer supports me in my life purpose to love and to bring love. It assists me to be present to each person with an open heart. It reinforces my intention to live authentically in relationship with others.

***

Over the years I have valued a number of disciplines and practices that have supported my journey. My journals have been invaluable companions in the maelstrom of life-changing events. I particularly appreciate the opportunity to connect with my 'internal little boy' and his pure wisdom and insight.

I do this by writing until I come to something I want to ask. I pose the question and then I take a pencil in my (non-preferred) left hand and wait for the spontaneous response to flow. It is often difficult to decipher what is written, so soon after I have finished I rewrite it with my right hand while I am able to recall what he has said. I am often stunned by the incisive clarity that he brings to my wondering.

Another journaling practice that I enjoy is writing for twenty minutes with a free-flowing stream of consciousness. (This is suggested by Julia Cameron in her book *The Artist's Way*. She calls it 'morning pages'.)

I rarely read what I have written. It's a record

of my rambling thoughts. It gets some junk out of the way, helps me to challenge self-defeating thoughts, and clears my mind for the day. Sometimes a fresh insight emerges and I gain a new clarity and perspective. I give myself a 'good talking to' at times.

Stillness and silence have been difficult disciplines for me to embrace but are becoming easier as I come closer to 'home'. I am learning to enjoy solitude, being in nature, sitting quietly in the bush, walking on the land, and being beside the ocean. The gentlest of breezes is a reminder of Spirit for me. When I stop and pay attention I hear an affirming declaration, sometimes in the softest movements of air.

You are loved.

I am valuing my own breath and its rhythms to ground me and bring me to centre, to bring me into my body. A well-used mantra – 'I am here now' – as I inhale and exhale has become a reliable friend. Listening to the wisdom of and paying attention to what my body is telling me is becoming a more trusted process for me. Paying attention. Paying attention. Paying attention. I have to practise this. Awareness and attention go together, reliable companions.

I walked today through a rocky landscape in the centre of Australia and wondered about significance. The landscape was formed 600 million years ago and has gradually been worn away to its current magnificence. It reminded me of those magical moments on a dark clear night when the stars fill the sky with their brilliance, and I feel so small. Significance, insignificance.

In such a vast and ancient universe, how significant am I? What about this moment in time? What about the length of my days?

My answer: This is who I am and what I have, now, and in this place. This body, this mind, these emotions, this life-force-erotic energy, this spirit. And I only have this moment. This moment will pass and the next moment is yet to arrive.

My resolve is to love and to bring love in this moment. I am closer to home. Home to my self, home to my own true nature. I return to it. I will trust it. It is home.

publisher

Do What Brings You Joy

Blaise van Hecke

My son often likes to talk about his childhood with me. It will start with something nostalgic – a food he liked or something the family did that seems bigger now than it did at the time because he has relived it in his memory.

As a parent this is heart-warming to hear him talk about this because we like to think that we create special memories for our children. Better still, many of these memories are of simple pleasures, such as making baked bean jaffles in an outdoor fire on holidays or skimming stones on the river or making fresh orange and pineapple juice on weekends. I made the fresh juice recently and when my son drank it, he enthusiastically told me how it takes him back to being a kid, and with joy he launched into a stream of reminiscence. In turn, I felt happiness at his sharing of these memories.

Each time we have these conversations, I feel warm and fuzzy. Then I think about my own childhood and the joy I had for many things, like reading a book, skimming stones on the river (passed on for a reason), swimming in the river, or eating my grandma's goulash. All of these things brought me joy then and continue to do so. Each time I experience that joy, my spirit is fuelled or topped up. It's as if the well is restocked with vital, life-sustaining substance.

As I've grown older, I've realised that refuelling my spirit is as important as maintaining my physical and mental health.

What is Spirit?

To have a conversation about 'spirit' means working out what the term means for each person. Is it about talking to people who have passed into the spirit world? This leads into conversations about death and dying and the afterlife. Or is it about faith and the religion that we follow? Both topics are big.

For me, spirit is my non-physical being. Who am I? My soul – or my essence, if you like – and how my spirit belongs to the world surrounding me. It is at once 'within' me and 'outside' of me. My 'being' connected to the universe.

The term 'spirit' is a greasy word thanks to so much religious history and debate. But what I have learned is that spirit is something that can't be measured, only felt, and that humans have an innate knowing about it. Not everyone acknowledges spirit but if it is ignored, our life can be less rich and less happy.

It is not realistic to separate mind, body and spirit into individual parts of our being because each has a direct effect on the other. It's all about balance. Unhappy mind leads to stomach issues which leads to physical disease which leads to dysfunction somewhere in the body which limits our relationships with each other which leads to unhappy emotions, and so on. It is important to look at all aspects of health, not just the physical. Therefore, our spiritual health is equally important. Unhappy spirit or soul leads to emotional unhappiness and so the cycle continues.

How do we find this harmony?
Spirit for me is HEART. The seat of our emotions. Look after your heart and your spirit will be healthy. By this I don't mean the physical heart but the emotional one. Do what makes your heart sing. Find joy in every day.

My joy is in storytelling. My life is immersed in story. I love hearing about other people, their lives, their passions, their failures. I love to learn about truth through these stories. From as far back as I can remember, I have loved books and writing stories and I now work with others to bring their stories into the world. This work involves creative process, just like my own writing is creation on a daily basis. Despite this, for many years I thought that writing was an indulgent activity and that I could not earn a living from it. This is how we are taught to think – that creative pursuits are time wasting and something to do in our down time. I have since learned that creation is vital to our health and that by doing it, we can increase our vibrations and create a healthy spirit.

Before I learned this valuable lesson, I took another vocational pathway. To earn a living, I decided to follow an aspiration to study natural medicine. I became a qualified massage therapist, and then went on to study naturopathy.

I had gone through my own physical dis-ease and found that many things improved when I ate better, did more exercise and lived more mindfully. Simple conclusions, but I liked the idea that I could help other people to heal themselves too.

For a variety of reasons, I had to give up my study (relationships, young children, lack of funds). At the time it was very disappointing but now I realise that it wasn't my true path.

I learned so much from my studies that I use in my life now that it was not a wasted effort. There are two measures of health that I incorporate into every day: homeostasis and higher vibrations.

Homeostasis is the body's constant striving for the right working environment. The perfect temperature, the perfect chemical balance, the perfect amount of fluids, etc.

When you get hot, you start sweating; when you're dehydrated, you drink fluid. Our body is always working hard at maintaining a homeostatic state and we should always be working at providing the right fuel, exercise, and environment to do this. It's obvious, then, if we drink too many sugary drinks, our chemical makeup will be affected. What will the body do to try to correct it?

Homeostasis is relatively easy to understand. It's common sense and really about living a balanced life and looking after our physical, mental and spiritual wellbeing.

The higher vibration may be harder to get our thoughts around. Dr Laws (my Naturopathic teacher) taught me that the higher our vibration, the better our health and wellbeing. This is physical, mental and spiritual.

Accordingly, the higher vibrational level you live at, the more joy, clarity and happiness you will have. It's a lightness of 'being'. Vibrations could be likened to energy or electricity.

Think about times when you have felt ill or run down, how the negative thoughts creep in and obstacles seem much bigger than normal. Low vibrations are linked to fear, anxiety, sadness, anger, and depression.

There are many ways to raise your vibration and, in a way, they are closely connected to homeostatic activity. Don't attempt to separate mind, body and spirit because each contributes to our homeostatic status.

Here are some activities that you can do that will raise your vibration:

- Body: Eat well, move your body, drink more water.
- Mind: Be mindful of your thoughts (negative thought creates negative reality), be grateful, be kind to other people and yourself.
- Spirit: Fill your life with beauty (joy), meditate, trust intuition.

There is nothing new about this list (and it isn't comprehensive) in creating a more balanced life, but not all of them are as easy to practice. The mind and spirit exercises are less tangible and will be harder for many to incorporate into their lives. As with anything, you must practice daily. It's not a matter of deciding to make changes and they happen purely by wanting it. It takes action, with purpose behind it.

My intention is not to lecture or be a health coach. I'm not qualified to do so. The above summary of healthy examples of living are to demonstrate that no matter what we do in our day-to-day lives, we can find ways to raise our vibrations and that will in turn give us a healthier spirit.

How does this relate to stories?

Have you ever been doing something that has allowed you to be totally lost in the moment, and you are so distracted that time becomes meaningless, shapeless or not measurable? This can happen often when we are caught up creating something. It comes from the pure joy of playing with something and being curious: cooking, gardening, colouring in, drawing, writing, painting, or whatever it is that interests you. As humans we are meant to create things and tell stories because it is a way for us to communicate with each other as well as articulate or make sense of the world we live in.

What does it mean to 'create' something? It means that a 'being' can take something physical and make something else from that using imagination to produce a work of art or an invention.

'But I don't have a creative bone in my body!' you might say.

This is a common statement I hear from people who don't work in creative industries. But I believe that EVERYONE can create something and find joy in the process – it's simply that they don't think laterally enough about it. The view is that 'creative' means being a good artist and that the finished product should have a value attached to it. Producing something out of your imagination is satisfying, joyful and healing on so many levels, so why not do something that is good for the soul?

My love of story is deeply ingrained in my being to the point of needing it every day. I will either read or write every single day. If I don't, I feel as though something is missing. It's almost a compulsion. A deep-seated need that will propel me forward.

Writing raises my vibration because I love doing it and it helps me to articulate my thoughts. You could say that it is a form of therapy for me.

Sometimes it feels like spirit is working through me. It isn't easy to articulate because it's an innate knowing. When living in a pure moment we are at once connected to the universe.

Joy is in us
So how do you find joy in your life? Just like my son, it might be worth visiting a time in your life when you felt happy. Make a list of all the things that bring you joy. The smallest of things can do this, like going out for coffee with someone or watching a movie. You may get joy from buying shiny new things like cars and handbags, but does that last? Is that sustainable? To check what does and doesn't bring you joy, try scoring your items. How much joy (how big is your smile) when you think about X, out of ten? As an example, when you think about your puppy, do you feel happy nine out of ten? When you listen to music, how do you feel?

If this exercise is hard, why not make a list of all the things you are grateful for? Make a list of at least ten. To help you get started, here's mine:

- I'm grateful for my strong, healthy body
- I'm grateful for my two healthy and happy sons
- I'm grateful for my long-term relationship
- I'm grateful for my cosy home
- I'm grateful for my dog, Oscar
- I'm grateful for my friendships
- I'm grateful for the freedom of my life
- I'm grateful for the beautiful city I live in
- I'm grateful for the food on my table
- I'm grateful for my positive attitude.

The above examples are broad but in thinking about them you will open pathways to your soul that you may have forgotten about. When I think about my dog, Oscar, I can't help but smile because I love his goofy personality and the fact that he is always living in the moment. Being with him moves me into being in the moment and brings me joy.

When you have your list of 'joyful' things, what then? Simple. Do them. You may feel silly doing some of them, others will come naturally. The joy you once felt for something may not return but have fun finding out. Be that child again if you have to. Be curious. Do whatever it takes to bring joy to your life, fill up your spirit. Do it often, replenish the well. You really can't have too much joy and life is too short to go without it.

mystic and yogini

Spirit is as Luminous as Your Awareness

Sally 'Lakshmi Amma' Thurley

I was born in Sweden to Aussie parents.
Then lived in the US.

Then Asia.

We didn't settle down permanently until my mother came back in '83.

That year, I was walking along the beach when something made me stop and look at my hands. In that moment, I instantly understood that I wasn't this body. I was eternal. Then I understood who I was and the role of karma. I also got that language creates the world and my experience. It was a random spontaneous awakening and the interesting thing is I was brought up in a Christian family – talk of karma, etc., wasn't heard of. This experience started my quest for that knowledge and wisdom.

At 16, at boarding school, when I heard a snippet of a Buddhist speaking, I knew I was going to live a spiritual life. By 25, I found the wisdom I craved. I met an enlightened being in an ashram and spent the next twenty years doing spiritual practice, yoga. Yoga is the pathway to a union with the divine. It's a philosophy and way of life; it is not a religion, although we did really enjoy the culture of its Vedic Indian roots. It also is most certainly not bending exercises in a gym class!

This wasn't an easy life path to follow. Life dished out many hard lessons. Being committed and devoted to self-realisation and wanting to understand the big questions of the universe with a spiritual community was like being in a fire of transformation. No part of it was easy.

But I did learn everything I needed to, and most especially, I learned about what Spirit is and how to nurture that relationship.

There is nothing more magnificent than Spirit – particularly being around someone with a healthy radiating presence of Spirit. We can all be that person with a little effort and understanding of what Spirit is and who we really are.

At our core, we are our source of origin. Consciousness. Still. Wise. Loving. Pure love.

This consciousness pulses and vibrates and manifests the universe. It becomes active, and creates. From a simplified mystical viewpoint, it is by the will of the divine that pure consciousness becomes form. This energetic process is called creation. This divine will is behind all creative processes we experience. It is not a 'God' figure that does this. It is inherent in the nature of consciousness itself.

In a magnificent dance of creation, this pure bliss consciousness begins to limit itself to become form, to individualise as us.

We are that pure bliss.

But we have become restricted in this body.

Imagine light pouring through a window on a sunny day. If you close the curtain, what happens? Depending on the curtain material, there may be a little loss of light, or a blackout. As beings of light this happens to us because of our minds. A mind that meditates, prays, and contemplates, thins the curtain and lets more light and more truth in.

> 'Ask yourself to whom this ignorance has come and you will discover that it never came to you and that you always have been Sat-chit-ananda (truth, consciousness, bliss). One goes through all sorts of austerities to become what one already is. All effort is simply to get rid of the mistaken impression that one is limited and bound by the woes of samsara (this life).'
>
> – Ramana Maharshi

We have been given this remarkable apparatus that sets us apart from all living creatures: the mind.

A good mind looks within. It inquires and begins the process of unbecoming, of going back home to source, which means going back home to us as our pure source of being, of nothing but consciousness.

A limited mind gets caught in the mundane of life, of being right, rational or irrational, and stuck in the conditioning of our society, family and our past.

We have become the servant of our minds and not the servants of the divine. The divine operates through our heart. We express the level we are at – emotionally, mentally and physically – through our actions.

But we have been given the opportunity to discover our source.

We can liberate and enlighten.

We can do this many ways, as is evident by the many wonderful faiths. Uniting the heart and the mind – the body and mind with Spirit – we are free from all limitations and it is the path of yoga which describes the means to unite with our God Self. The God Self is our mind beyond the ego mind, a big mind that is the witness of life and is not impacted by life.

There is limitation, then there are the means to liberation. The methods can be sweet and intense, or straightforward and complicated, depending on our natures and what we need and are attracted to. They are the key to a healthy spirit, and to healing what is perceived as an unhealthy spirit – although, in truth, there is no such thing because Spirit is pure consciousness.

What judges and categorises the state of our individual or collective spirit? Our mind.

Contemplate, though, that the mind is also a manifestation of Spirit. What we see or perceive as negative is as much made of spirit consciousness as what we judge positive. The limitation is in our understanding.

How our lives and minds have manifested depends on what we do with the conditioning we have in regards to the actions and choices we have made – in other words, our karma. What we choose to do to get back to Spirit is our dharma.

Dharma is the law of the universe that keeps everything in harmony. There is always harmony in chaos. Everything and everyone has a place and a purpose and no one is ever left out. When we live with integrity and heart, with responsibility, we work to keep harmony and do what we love doing, we are living 'dharmically.'

> 'The very activity of the mind is a barrier to its own understanding.'
>
> – J Krishnamurti.

Grace is another word for consciousness. Grace is alive, bestowing, active and mysterious. Grace is mystical. It has the power to remind us that we are Spirit. It is the same light shining through the window. Through grace's own will, it can reveal itself or keep itself concealed, so it can also be the curtain.

Grace is also love as healing energy. We all have the same amount of grace open to us and we can harness it to work on our behalf. Spending time with people with a big spirit or established in grace can open the curtain and our hearts.

A healthy spirit is one that has found a way to shine through us. We have allowed it to radiate by purifying or removing the filters, the blocks of energy or ignorance that have come from our experiences, emotions, and desires. All we need is the intention to do so and to focus on Spirit – this means to turn within and take the time necessary to get to know one's Self. Meditation is the finest and easiest method. Establishing a consistent meditation routine that suits you – particularly under the supervision of a good teacher – will always bear fruit. Make sure the teacher has the presence of Spirit and grace you are after, otherwise the practice may be dry and unyielding.

We need to start to recognise Spirit. Many people ask me if I can prove to them that there is divinity and Spirit. I respond by saying that there is nothing that isn't Spirit – show me where Spirit isn't. If they come from an understanding that there is nothing, that there is merely matter in this world, we are born and we die, then the best thing for me to do is to give them a warm, loving smile, let grace do its thing, and leave them with that.

They focus too much on the limited view that comes from some kinds of religion, that there is a god in the skies who pours grace on those who believe and are good and damns those who don't and are not. This mentality feeds the problem and shows a lack of understanding from real experience.

When we box creation like this, we are not able to see the full picture and we get caught up in arguments that keep us in a loop of ignorance. New Age theories can slip into this age-old conditioning too. Good and bad. Duality. Put all of these aside and keep a broad, loving and universal approach. Remember, consciousness is love and it is Spirit, and we are all at different stages of awakening and awareness of our true nature.

I find it helpful to approach it like this: when we go through this creative process of becoming, as we start to take on our human existence and become part of this universe, we become part of the nature of it. Hence, we forget our true nature in the process. Deep down, there is a part of us that remembers that we are Spirit, and it recognises where we come from.

In the wisdom I studied and participated in for many years, we learned that at the initial point of individualising from universal consciousness is the stuff of the universe. Behind everything we see and can't see is consciousness.

We first experience being no longer whole. We have forgotten who we are and feel that we are not enough, not safe, limited: this is the core of our negative beliefs. For many, this can play out as anxiety, depression and pain.

That's why I recommend meditation, just sitting and being with your awareness, learning to feel the feelings of home, of wholeness and joy. Sitting with full acceptance that we are divine and we are universal consciousness, then we go back to harmony and unity. This is possible. When we cease to see anything as good or bad, when we accept everything as it is, we heal and we experience the fullness of Spirit.

My teacher used to say that the ultimate suffering is poverty of Shakti – spirit or grace. You could also say it is having no idea of one's connection with the spirit that is always flowing through them. Not knowing where there is a lot of grace and where there is little, and how to move in the right direction. Not understanding how to follow the clear space of good feeling, and having trust and faith in our relationship with the cosmos and our innate wisdom and intuition.

A healthy spirit is about becoming whole and merging all aspects of our being that we may have neglected or pushed away. A great soul has a free loving heart, an open discerning mind and uses the body as a vehicle for service to humanity. When we pay attention to these areas, we find out what requires attention, what muscle we may need to build. We are all born predominantly stronger in one area and need to work during our lifetime to integrate and bring harmony and flow between those three areas.

All cultures and faiths have their version of practices that free our spirit and give us a rich, fulfilled life. Scientific studies also back these up. Make your list of what you already do, can do more of and learn new skills in. In some way they all have dharma, a way to live responsibly and in harmony with the world around us, in making the most of our relationships, roles, gifts and our connection to God.

Let me start with the heart, our centre of infinite intelligence. If love is infinite intelligence, then wisdom gives it expression and dharma gives it legs. Cool, huh?

At the ashram, we were taught that spirituality is merely being able to welcome another with love. That's it. It has nothing to do with wearing robes, shaving your head, reading scriptures or playing with crystals. If you can greet everyone with love, regardless of your circumstances, you are the healthiest spirit. That means without agenda, judgment, expectations and so forth.

> 'The heart is the hub of all sacred places. Go there and roam.'
>
> – Bhagawan Nityananda

A heart that can do this has faith in a loving and supportive universe. There is an ability to clear hurt, to forgive and not indulge in the destructive nature of a grudge. When we forgive from 'the bottom of our heart', the deepest recesses of it, then we free ourselves and others from a life less lived: from bondage, disease and disempowerment.

The only area in our life we need to truly declutter – especially for a healthy spirit – is our heart. We need to check in with it daily and ask, 'Is there anyone or anything in here that needs attention?' Forgiving is healing and freedom. You still love a person and yet you do what you need to do to keep on your journey, whether with them or not. You need to put to sleep issues that take up a lot of mental RAM in your subconscious mind that cause anxiety and stress – issues that block us from healthy spirit.

Healing means attention and focus. Something has cried out and caused some discomfort in the effort for recognition. It is a visitor on our path and wants some time. No matter what it is, we need always to honour that which has knocked on our door, like how in India they relate to visitors always with generosity and kindness – the visitor coming to our door could be Krishna or God in disguise.

We see all as visitors who deserve our love. If we can keep a detached mood and observe, we can shift any energy. When we have the intention of holding a space of loving grace and not seeing anything as good or bad, we can heal. Healing is a soul thing, a spirit thing. It is not the body. Whether this body stays or perishes is not the point. We do whatever it takes to let the spirit shine and most often than not, in that process we heal on the material plane.

The best way to do this, again, is meditation. Sit with the issues that want healing. Go to where it is in your body – or if you understand energy centres, go there – and, as you breathe, visualise life force and healing energy going to that area. The breath alone will do. Focus and meditate for as long as is needed and that area will shift.

> 'Contemplation of the inner Self frees the individual from his suffering and feeling of limitation.'
>
> – Shiva Sutras

I understand healing and suffering. Sometimes, I think the fact I was born a mystic with an early awakening set me up for a life of experiencing pain. I've been crushed enough to have so much compassion for our humanness.

I remember going through a process where I wanted to fully understand it from the outside in. I'd accepted, done the work and yet still here I was – all this spiritual practice and living, but still feeling suffering. I knew what it was on an academic level, but I also knew that until it was something that came from deep inside me, I would never conquer it.

One day, I was at a program with my spiritual teacher who remarked that suffering – according to Eastern philosophy – was ignorance. I knew this. Where was the ignorance? Of course, the answer is in the question. Ignorance is concealment of grace. I get that now I'm out the other side. So how did I get there?

'Suffering is when we don't have what we want,' he continued.

Bingo. Light bulb. I took that away and contemplated it and my life for a few days. How is that relevant to the nature of spirit and manifestation? How does it tie into Kashmir Shaivism, which is the philosophy and way of life I grew up in?

'Kashmir Shaivism' is a non-dual philosophy that originated in the Kashmir region of India that says we are one and never separate from 'God' or universal consciousness. It is non-religious, dogmatic, restrictive. It is for the every day person and teaches essentially that we can all see 'Shiva,' or consciousness, in every aspect of life. When that happens, we are liberated. Kashmir Shaivisim is the earliest teachings of cosmic vibration.

One day, after locking myself in my workspace for a day, I got it. The answer came when I happened upon a picture of four concentric circles. These represented what is called a 'mandala'.

A mandala is simply a circle – a circle is complete and whole. It represents enlightenment and oneness. With concentric circles we can visualise steps that can lead us to the outer circle or back to the inner circle. It was a map, a science of self-realisation. At that moment, I came up with a new distinction of what it is we want and why. It sounds trippy, but it was just one of those 'grace' moments where everything made sense.

***

We not only push away what we don't want and get too attached to what we think we do want that we forget that we are here to go home. Home is enlightenment. Freedom. Enlightenment is what we all want and crave on a soul level. Once we start to meditate we begin to experience this.

It is always inside of us – a deep inner knowing that we are whole and complete. We know we come from somewhere, which is why we get sad, anxious and depressed in life. Often, those mental states aren't that there's something wrong, it's that we are longing for home, for rest, for peace. Enlightenment is simply going home while still alive. You work it all out.

We are Spirit. So what is Spirit? What are the qualities of the divine? Love, happiness, joy, wisdom, abundance, peace. Like the sun through the curtain, sometimes it can be blocked, but the sun is always shining, and Spirit is always flowing through us. We are what we already want. All we have to do is know how to move our mundane worldly wants to that of Spirit. I turned it into a process, and that is the breakthrough work I help people with. We can move towards our true nature every day if we prioritise it and are aware of our spirit, or what I call our *soul wants*. Then we can start to transcend and transform this earthly experience to one that is heavenly.

As with the heart, the mind also needs attention. Part of this begins with language – and not the sort people think was created from us grunting as apes.

If the universe was created by sound, by the word – which the Bible also says – then there must be more to it. There is. Sanskrti is such a language. Language moving to a higher place is someone who's aware of what they say. They work on their mindset, on being positive, on self love, on seeing and expressing things as their soul would, not the negative, judgemental, nasty thoughts that inhabit the minds of most people which totally determine the quality of their life.

Learning the mystical nature of language and catching our regular thought habits and moving them to the highest form of language, to Spirit, turns the mind into Spirit. This can be through meditation, chanting the names of the divine, mindset and work. Self-inquiry is the king of spiritual tools. No matter what is happening, always go back to the origin of the feeling, thought or reaction, go back to the source by asking the question, *Who am I?* There are many self-inquiry techniques, and that alone can heal and take you to enlightenment swiftly.

There is always love in action or dharma. We are here to be of service to humanity. We are here to know our true nature and the gifts we have been given in order to use them for the good of all. That is dharma. We are supposed to be active and we all have a purpose for being here. Often, our lives heal and our spirit shines when we come to this understanding.

This is the most beautiful example of Spirit – human spirit. We are all sacred, and we are all mysterious as we are pure grace. Nurture human spirit and watch your spirit soar.

Be of service, help others. Service can be in the form of selfless service to a community or organisation that do good work in the world. It may be by starting your own humanitarian work, or it could be volunteering your time to a local company that needs your support, like an aged care facility or kids holiday program.

Instead of getting stuck in your own head go out and find a person that needs help more than you. Help a friend declutter their wardrobe, cook your neighbour dinner, see a friend in the hospital.

The human spirit is more evident and impressive during times of collective struggle, yet there are acts of human spirit – that make the world a place of peace and functionality – that are happening all the time, every day, without recognition or reward. Without it, there would be less flow.

Compassion is the loveliest expression of human spirit. Being present with each other, listening and acknowledging without getting emotionally drawn into another's story. What a gift we all have, the ability to give. We learn so much about our spirit and nature when we are present with one another, especially when we have no need to solve, correct or influence.

Be a contributor or a leader, take a stand for humanity and grace. I run free public programs to support spirit and humanity – meditation, chanting, discussion of spiritual topics, creating a community that supports each other, going out and socialising and online. It's my responsibility to do so. I believe that the real 80/20 rule is 80% of what you do daily is loving and giving, and the other 20% is that which provides you with the time and money to do it. It is possible. I call it spiritual entrepreneurship.

I love to support people in working out how they can take their spiritual nature to the world, to lead towards a peaceful and enlightened society and to thrive personally as well. Old school religious purists may have difficulty with that idea, but it is all a part of the evolution of consciousness and what is needed today.

Enlightenment is the goal of life. It is where we all inevitably choose to focus. When the time is right, it will call you and there is nothing you can do about it. When we free ourselves, we free all. We get there by allowing the evolution of our spirit to take place.

If you are getting the call of Spirit, then listen. It is important to note, that as beneficial as giving is, if we are unable to receive graciously then we are not really giving. They need to be equal and mutually inclusive. Ego can have difficulties receiving or sometimes giving, but if it is always going in one direction, then there is an imbalance.

> 'In which state this whole universe is existing, that is the real sense the reality of being.'
>
> – Spanda Karikas

Merge with the divine. Move to that which is behind our attachments and aversions, our thoughts, feelings and actions. Discover the unified feeling of oneness. Feel the bliss. Remember, you are perfect. We all have the ability to unite with Spirit. We all have the capacity to digest the ills of life and move a negative state to a positive state. We need to know how we have lost the art of living and focusing on a healthy spirit.

This book is evidence there is a movement back to more robust spiritual discussion and education. Ponder profoundly mystical truth. Know that you are the light and anchor yourself in grace. Make this your goal in life and I assure you, you will have the most magnificent spirit that can heal and reveal the same spirit in all who are ready to be it too.

Biographies

Joffa Corfe works for the Salvation Army and volunteers for the Epilepsy Foundation of Victoria, Reclink Australia and Hepatitis Victoria, amongst others.

Joffa's personal religious view is, 'Treat others as you'd wish to be treated.'

One of his greatest loves is the community of football and how it can bring different personalities all together.

Arna Delle-Vergini is a barrister keeping it real with her three kids and a dog in the northern burbs of Melbourne.

Arna specializes in children's law and family violence and also sits on the Mental Health Tribunal of Victoria.

In an alternate reality, Arna writes fantasy fiction for children and young adults. When she grows up she would like to live an ordinary, uneventful life.

After completing a Bachelor Degree in Science (majoring in chemistry and biochemistry) at Sydney University, **Kylie Hennessy** began teaching yoga.

Kylie practiced intensely in various forms of yoga such as Okido Yoga, Ki Yoga and Ashtanga Yoga while completing four-year apprenticeship style of training with Body Mind Unlimited in Sydney to teach Hatha Yoga.

From then her life was all about yoga, meditation and healing modalities. Over many years, Kylie explored the chakra system and energy reading – in particular, the amazing healing qualities of the heart chakra with Karima Hinterleitner, long-term follower of the enlightened Mystic Osho.

Kylie worked closely and trained with Traditional Chinese Medicine Practitioner, tai chi and Qi Gong teacher Anegla Zhu, and trained with Japanese Yoga teachers such as Peter Masters of Zen Central and Jack Marshall of Zen Renaissance Centre. She has also studied with many of Australia's leading yoga therapists.

She enjoys the work of scientists such as Dr Candice Pert, Dr Bruce Lipton and Dr Jo Dispenza, whose work compliments her own knowledge and experience of yoga.

The sum of this experience has expanded into running three yoga studios and natural health clinics across Sydney and at the Sydney Pregnancy Centre. The centre warmly welcomes all kinds of people to enjoy a range of yoga classes, yoga therapy and other mind-body therapies offering a place of healing, community and support.

Eric Hudson is a dad with four children and nine grandchildren who works as a trauma counsellor.

He has been in professional roles where his participation has helped to promote kindness and safety in relationships.

He has been particularly interested in supporting men with histories of violence in re-discovering their essential nature as kind, loving and safe participants in their own, and others' lives.

His work as a counsellor has given him the understanding of the way that trauma plays out in people's lives.

Anthony Kilner is a psychic medium, multi-published author, educational facilitator, mentor, energy worker, freelance photojournalist, speaker and musician.

He is also qualified in trance healing, massage and is a Reiki and Seichim Master. Having studied vibrational healing and meditation techniques in India and Australia, Anthony understands these to be powerful tools to promote ongoing wellbeing that work on the entire physical body and encourage self-healing.

In 2018 Anthony also launched *Bridging Realms – Core Issue Vibrational Healing*™. This system of energy work combines everything Anthony has learnt over the last 25 years into a single package, offering a unique holistic service for his clients.

Anthony has also created a beautiful working and teaching environment in Research Victoria where he operates his businesses – Bridging Realms – www.bridgingrealms.com.au, Ant e Fiction and The Spiritual Coach.

Anthony is passionate about assisting people with a holistic approach to living and working and how to find the right work/life balance. In 2013 he started his newest business, The Spiritual Coach, and also wrote his first book, *Secret*

Spiritual Business – Unlocking the Power to Holistic Success, where he shares a plethora of knowledge and personal experiences on how to achieve success while doing what you love and working from home.

Anthony collaborated in the first of the Health Conscious trilogy of co-authored books starting with *Healthy Mind* in 2015. This was followed by *Healthy Body* in 2017. With the launch of *Healthy Spirit* (2018) Anthony's written work combines a very different spiritual take on understanding what a healthy spirit or Soul is, and how to find it. It's the trilogy that creates the trinity of mind, body & spirit!

His latest book, *Practical Mediumship – A Guide to Understanding Psychics, Mediums, Dreams and Physical and Metaphysical Information,* covers in greater detail the world of Subjective and Objective information, dream interpretation and more, rounding out a great package of books he has on offer.

Catholic Priest Fr **Bob Maguire** has a long history working with the poorest and most marginalised in Melbourne's community. He is a pioneer in the social sector.

Fr Bob's early life instilled in him a sense of care and concern for the forgotten members of community, the 'unlovely and the unloved'. Bob led the Character Training Unit for young officers in the Australian Army before beginning his well-known 39 year stint as parish priest of St Peter and Paul Church in South Melbourne.

This is where his outreach work took hold and really grew. He threw himself into the service of the homeless and those down on their luck. He worked with anyone – criminal, addicted, young and old could rely on him.

His latest venture, The Fr Bob Maguire Foundation was launched in 2003.

Now in his mid 80s, he is currently actively engaged in the Fr Bob Maguire Foundation – an organisation that served more than 40,000 hot meals and around 10,000 hampers this year and growing, along with Outreach and Counselling to over 5000 clients to date.

While also driving his Education fund to support our local youth with scholarships for secondary education, one of his dreams is to help beyond and see that our young thrive.

Mary Jo McVeigh is the founder and CEO of Cara House and CaraCare. Mary Jo is acknowledged in her field as an expert in child protection, trauma therapy, clinical supervision, management training, leadership coaching, facilitation, and professional self-care with over 25 years working with both the public and private sectors.

Mary Jo completed her Honours degree in social science in 1983 and worked in her community of North Belfast before returning to university and completing a Master's Degree in Social Work in 1986. Mary Jo is currently undertaking a PHD in Social Work at Sydney University.

Mary Jo is a trained trauma therapist and an accredited mental health social worker with a passion for inspiring people to optimise their full potential. She is particularly skilled at working with professionals to bring about growth, notably in the areas of leadership, effectiveness, and communication.

Mary Jo draws on her vast knowledge and experience in trauma and protection to lift and inspire her audiences.

As a passionate writer, Mary Jo has also authored *Without Question, the Language of the Mindful leader and Audacious Love.* She has also published three innovative resources for working therapeutically with children and young people.

The most beloved one, Wrapped in Angels, has received praise nationally and internationally. Mary Joy enjoys writing as a relaxation tool which inspires her to write poetry, books and journal articles.

Jenny Mitchell is an Australian civil marriage celebrant. She has been performing marriage and other ceremonies in Victoria, New South Wales and the ACT for over twelve years.

Jenny realised early on that celebrancy combined many of her interests – writing, civil service and romantic comedies – and so she trained as a celebrant at the age of only twenty-four.

Jenny writes personalised ceremonies for each and every occasion over which she presides. She finds enormous sparkle and verve in the love and life stories she hears from Australians from all walks of life celebrating significant milestones.

While she has conducted many weddings, her favourite is still the one at which she met her now-husband (she figured they didn't call him the Best Man for nothing).

Jenny is also a proud public servant, makes an award-winning coconut ice, and compiles cryptic crosswords for cheap thrills.

Sally 'Lakshmi Amma' Thurley is a mystic and recognised spiritual teacher in her tradition who is driven to help people awaken to who they are, become anchored in that awareness and take that experience to transform and heal the world.

Her message is 'Big Mind, Big Heart, Big Being'. Spirituality is meant to be simple. She is a published author of the book the *She-Monk: Daily Life is the New Spiritual Practice* and *Mastering Your Inner Game*.

After spending decades studying and participating in non-dual Eastern wisdom philosophy with an ashram, Sally has learned how to merge spiritual practice, self-awareness, personal development and service to humanity with a compassionate b.s.-free universal approach.

Sally works with mindfulness in corporate business and also runs courses on philosophy, spiritual development and leadership and has her own spiritual community the Self Knowledge Sangha running regular programs.

She is very keen on what is feminine leadership in this new era and establishing an avenue for women to be the new leaders, teachers, visionaries and healers using the knowledge and skills provided by spirituality and her yoga – Spandashakti Yoga.

Email sallyshemonk@gmail.com, to get her signature meditation to discover your soul's want. Or if you'd like more information visit www.sallythurley.com.

Blaise van Hecke is co-owner Busybird Publishing. She is also a writer, photographer and artist.

She has been published in the short story anthology, *Mud Puddles* (May 08), *Blue Crow Magazine*, *[untitled]* issue two, came second in the bi-annual short story competition with the Society of Women Writers of Victoria 2007, for her story 'The Eleventh Summer'; and is the author of *The Book Book: 12 steps to successful publishing*, as well as

Who is a Cheeky Monkey?. Her latest book, *The Road to Tralfamadore is Bathed in River Water,* is a collection of stories from her childhood living on a commune in the 70s.

Blaise enjoys writing and travelling and hopes to publish a book that combines both. She runs various workshops for Busybird about writing, editing, and publishing, and is popularly in demand for talks about publishing in general.

What Blaise loves most is nurturing an author through the self-publishing process, and the look on their face when they finally have their book in their hands.

Find out more about Blaise at www.thebookchick.com.au.

Title: *Healthy Mind*
Series: The HealthConscious Project
Price: $25.00
Publication Date: 23 October 2015
Format: Paperback (210x135mm, 182 pages)
ISBN: 978 1 925260 78 8
Category: Nonfiction

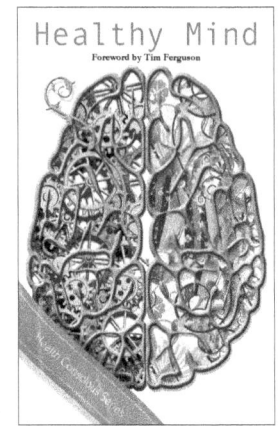

How do you keep a healthy mind?

In the hustle and bustle of our everyday lives, it's a question that's often neglected. We may diet or exercise to take care of our bodies, but little thought is given to good mental health. Mental health issues – things like depression, anxiety, etc. – are on the rise. A general malaise of constant tiredness, agitation, or even anger, is common.

How do you feel? As you read this blurb, pause a moment and reflect on your mental health. Is your outlook positive, constructive, and purposeful? Or do you find yourself often flustered, uptight, and confused? Unfortunately, we can run with these patterns so long they become our mindset. But surely you want something better. Surely you deserve something better?

Healthy Mind features articles from ten diverse professionals who explore the concept of a healthy mind from their specific viewpoint, and offer tips and exercises on creating and maintaining good mental health.

Simple, interesting, and compelling, *Healthy Mind* has something for everybody, and is sure to become an invaluable guide.

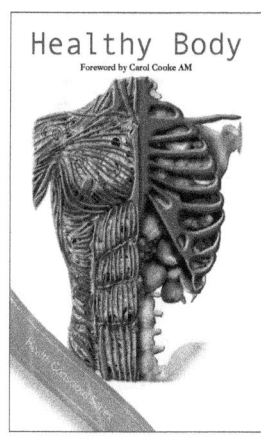

Title: *Healthy Body*
Series: The HealthConscious Project
Price: $25.00
Publication Date: 22 July 2017
Format: Paperback (210x135mm, 208 pages)
ISBN: 978-1-925585-57-5
Category: Nonfiction

How do you keep a healthy body?

There are so many differing opinions about how to keep our body healthy and at peak performance. So many diets, so many physical activities to take part in.

How do you feel? Close your eyes and take a mental scan of your body. Are there aches and pains? Is your digestion a bit off today? Do you struggle to get started each day, moaning as you throw the covers back each morning?

Healthy Body features articles from ten non-competing professionals who explore the concept of a healthy body from their specific viewpoint, and offer tips and exercises on creating and maintaining good physical health.

These articles are meant to be simple, interesting and useful to you. No medical jargon or complex ideas that you have to decipher before you can use them. Healthy Body has something for everybody, an invaluable guide that you can dip in and out of.

With a Foreword written by gold-medal paralympian Carole Cooke.

Pinion Press is an imprint of Busybird Publising, specialising in publishing a handful of our own titles yearly, trying to combine quality and enjoyability with some altruistic outcome, e.g. raising awareness for a particular condition (as our glorious coffee table photography book, *Walk With Me* – a journal of Kev Howlett's trek up to Mount Everest Base Camp and back – raised awareness of Charcot-Marie-Tooth disease), and/or donate a portion of proceeds for books to various foundations (such as Women Helping Women, Breast Cancer Victoria, the Prostate Cancer Foundation, the Epilepsy Foundation, Vision Australia, and the Indigenous Literacy Foundation.

Busybird Publishing is a boutique micropublisher based in the heart of Montmorency, Victoria.

We help authors self-publish. A fee-for-service self-publisher, we make no claims on rights or royalties, and are determined that to make sure our authors have a pleasurable, gratifying, and educational journey.

We also run workshops on various forms of writing (fiction, nonfiction, memoir), publishing, and photography, and an annual two-day writing retreat; host a monthly Open Mic Night (the third Wednesday of every month); and hold competitions to help aspiring writers get published or win mentoring.

To learn more about Busybird Publishing, check out our website at **www.busybird.com.au**.

www.ingramcontent.com/pod-product-compliance
Lightning Source LLC
LaVergne TN
LVHW011940070526
838202LV00054B/4732